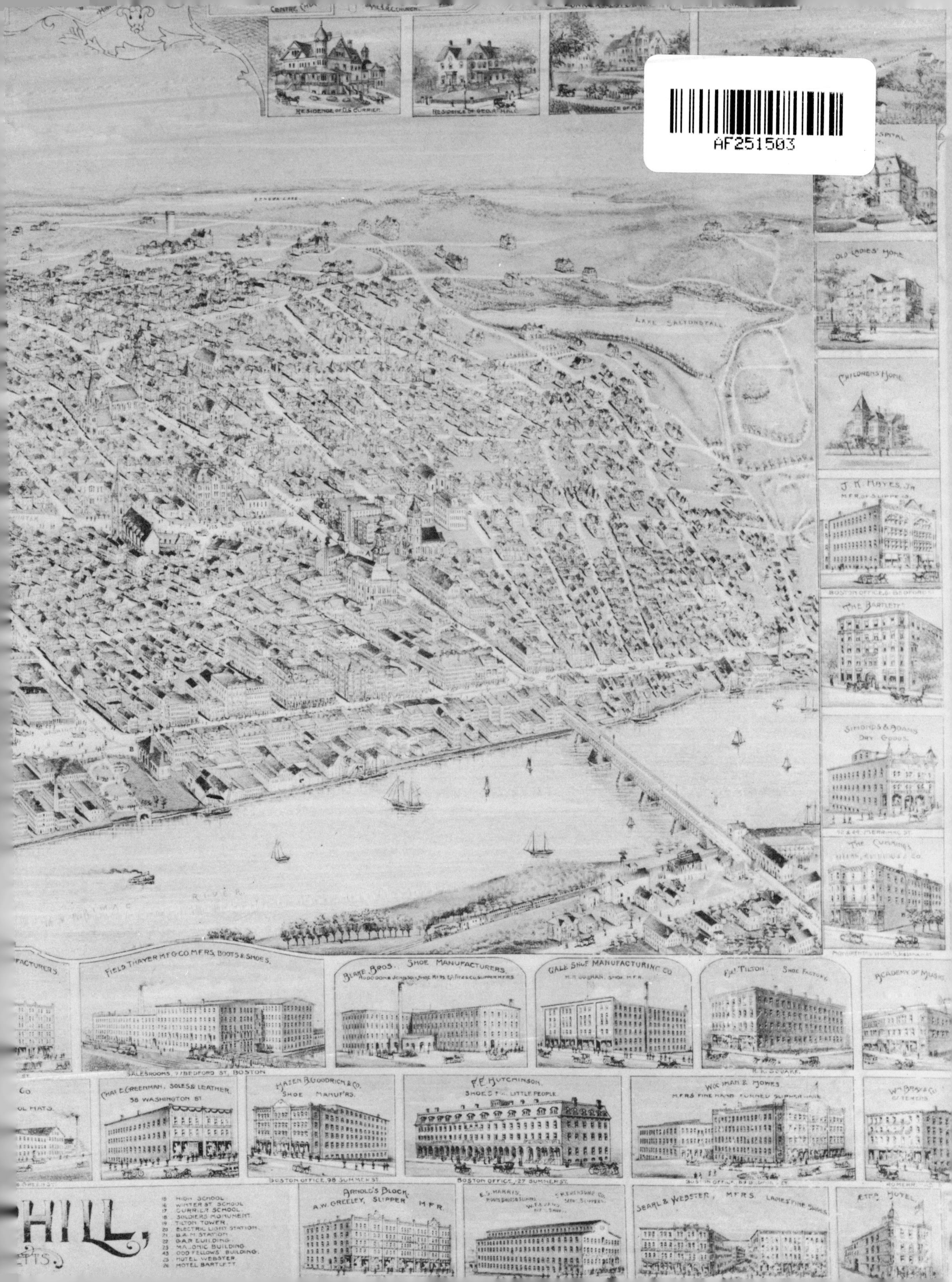

RESIDENCE OF D.S. CURRIER
RESIDENCE OF GEO. A. HALL
KENOZA LAKE
LAKE SALTONSTALL
HOSPITAL
OLD LADIES' HOME
CHILDREN'S HOME
J.K. HAYES, JR. MFR. OF SLIPPERS
THE BARTLETT
SIMONDS & ADAMS DRY GOODS
THE CUSHMAN
MERRIMAC RIVER
FIELD THAYER MFG. CO. MFRS. BOOTS & SHOES.
BLAKE BROS. SHOE MANUFACTURERS.
GALE SHOE MANUFACTURING CO.
E.A. TILTON SHOE FACTORY
ACADEMY OF MUSIC
SALESROOMS, 77 BEDFORD ST. BOSTON
CHAS. E. GREENMAN, SOLES & LEATHER. 38 WASHINGTON ST.
HAZEN B. GOODRICH & CO. SHOE MANUF'RS.
BOSTON OFFICE, 98 SUMMER ST.
F.E. HUTCHINSON. SHOES FOR LITTLE PEOPLE.
BOSTON OFFICE, 27 SUMMER ST.
WOCKMAN & HOWES MFRS. FINE HAND TURNED SLIPPERS
WM. BRAY & CO.
HILL,
MASSACHUSETTS.
15 HIGH SCHOOL
16 WINTER ST. SCHOOL
17 CURRIER SCHOOL
18 SOLDIERS MONUMENT
19 TILTON TOWER
20 ELECTRIC LIGHT STATION
21 B.&M. STATION
22 G.A.R. BUILDING
23 MASONIC BUILDING
24 ODD FELLOWS BUILDING
25 HOTEL WEBSTER
26 HOTEL BARTLETT
ARNOLD'S BLOCK. A.W. GREELEY, SLIPPER MFR.
E.S. HARRIS
SEARL & WEBSTER, MFRS. LADIES FINE SHOES

HAVERHILL
MASSACHUSETTS

Produced in cooperation with
Bradford College
and the Greater Haverhill Chamber of Commerce

Windsor Publications, Inc.
Northridge, California

A New England City

HAVERHILL

MASSACHUSETTS

AN ILLUSTRATED HISTORY BY
PATRICIA TRAINOR O'MALLEY
& PAUL H. TEDESCO

Windsor Publications, Inc.—
History Book Division

Vice President, Publishing: Hal
  Silverman
Editorial Director: Teri Davis
  Greenberg
Design Director: Alexander
  D'Anca

Staff for *A New England City:
Haverhill, Massachusetts*

Editors: Gail Koffman, Dianne
  Woo
Picture Editor: Lynne Chapman
Director, Corporate Biographies:
  Karen Story
Assistant Director, Corporate
  Biographies: Phyllis Gray
Proofreader: Susan J. Muhler
Editor, Corporate Biographies:
  Brenda Berryhill
Editorial Assistants: Kathy M.
  Brown, Susan Kanga, Pat
  Pittman, Jeffrey Reeves
Sales Representative: Mary
Whelan
Layout Artist, Corporate
  Biographies: Mari Catherine
  Preimesberger
Layout Artist, Editorial: Susan L.
  Wells
Designer: Lori Sandler

Library of Congress Cataloging-in-Publication Data

O'Malley, Patricia Trainor, 1937-
    A New England city : Haverhill, Massachusetts : an illustrated
history / by Patricia Trainor O'Malley and Paul H. Tedesco. —
1st ed.
      p.   cm.
    Bibliography: p. 124
    Includes index.
    ISBN 0-89781-218-2
    1. Haverhill (Mass.)—History. 2. Haverhill (Mass.)—Description
—Views. 3. Haverhill (Mass.)—Industries. I. Tedesco, Paul H.
II. Title.
F74.H5052   1987   87-20913
974.4'5—dc19   CIP

Previous page: *As Haverhill expanded to the west, especially in the River Street area, promotion was undertaken to convince potential industrialists and residents of the virtues of the community. Green hills and farm land were to be found, as seen in this 1889 view of the area surrounding the prosperous and expansive city along the Merrimack. Lithograph by the Bufford Lithograph Company, Boston. Courtesy, Trustees of the Haverhill Public Library*

CONTENTS

PROLOGUE

H e sat before an open window, his motions in plain view of the people on Washington Street three stories below. It was an unbroken routine, methodical and efficient: Pick up a shoe from the left pile, move it to the lasting machine in front of him, and place it on the right pile. The noise of his machine cut through the air. On an unseasonably warm day in October 1985, this lone worker sat in Lesande Shoe Company, the last operating shoe shop in Haverhill, Massachusetts.

Two doors west stood another building. Intricate metal scaffolding covered its facade. Newly cleaned brick and paneless windows drew the observer's eye, the whine of power saws and the blows of hammers distracted the ear. Brightly painted signs reminded passersby of the luxury apartments and offices soon to open there.

Less than 50 feet separated these two buildings, but more than 50 years separated their activities. The solitary laster represented the final spark of life in an industry that had been moribund for more than half a century. Nearly 100 years ago every building on Washington Street and on blocks north and west of it teemed with shoeworkers. Now, the ongoing renovations anticipated the advent of a new population of engineers, technicians, academics, artists, doctors, and lawyers. In place of the laster's staccato drill, the air would soon reverberate with the sound of expensive stereo systems and personal computers.

The air that October day vibrated with vitality. A new life had come to downtown Haverhill, one that fit into old buildings like a rightful heir.

New ways fitting comfortably with the old, and remnants of the past beside the structures of the present—this is the image that Haverhill projects in the final decades of the twentieth century. Haverhill is unique among the cities of the Merrimack Valley. It is an industrial city with a high-tech future built on a colonial past. The effect has been a layering of eras: Eighteenth-century farmhouses and nineteenth-century factories share space with

A horse-drawn trolley first operated in Haverhill in 1877, after which the system rapidly grew, providing public transportation throughout the greater Haverhill area. Most routes were electrified beginning in 1892. The system continued until 1936, when the last routes were replaced with buses. This 1905 photo of Arlington Street, taken from Main Street, shows two boys hopping on for a free ride—a popular activity for decades. Courtesy, Trustees of the Haverhill Public Library

twentieth-century condominiums, and an interstate highway cuts across a landscape whose contours determined seventeenth-century pathways.

Haverhill was established in the seventeenth century as a colonial river port. In the late nineteenth century the city was dubbed the Queen Slipper City when its cottage shoe production grew into a huge industry. Now, some 350 years after its incorporation, Haverhill is still changing; in the spirit of survival, the town is again attempting to meet the needs of the region's next economic cycle.

Historians have pointed to New England to show that economic growth can be sustained despite a rigorous climate and the land's lack of natural bounty. Early industrial development in the region was aided by direct access to world markets through the port of Boston; creative immigrants who designed machinery and developed production methods; availability of quality waterpower; and a transportation network that reached the expanding West.

From 1820-1860 New England became the most industrialized region of the nation, and Haverhill itself continued to flourish despite the reduction of foreign imports during the Civil War and the relocation of industries to the South and to the West during the twentieth century.

Shoemaking and Haverhill were synonomous for more than 100 years. Until the 1850s, shoe leather was cut in buildings along Water Street and then sent to the countryside, where farm families operating out of small structures called "ten-footers" would sew the leather into shoes. The finished products were returned to the shoe manufacturer, paid for in cash or goods, and sent on to American and European markets. By the 1860s the invention of machinery made it possible to centralize shoe production. Factories were built from White's Corner to Railroad Square.

Individuality and civic pride were abundant. Unlike its great industrial neighbors upriver, Lawrence and Lowell, Haverhill chose to build smaller factories, which permitted attention and care in the shoe industry that were never a part of large-scale textile production. During the last decade of the nineteenth century, the Victorian 1890s, the quantity and quality of Haverhill's shoe production earned the city its nickname of Queen Slipper City of the World.

After World War I, the industry was weakened by the importation of cheap shoes, by the location of factories to areas that were both nearer to raw materials and free of labor unions, and by the inability or unwillingness of local manufacturers to adjust to changes in an extremely cyclical industry. The depression of the 1930s definitively ended the golden days of Haverhill's shoe industry.

With the decline of local industry, Washington Street, which has risen from the ashes of the great fire of 1882, degenerated and developed a very unsavory reputation. The cafes turned into bars, the nights became dangerous, and the street grew dirty and neglected. Then, when all seemed lost, the faith of a few individuals and the nation's rediscovery of itself through a massive preservation movement set the stage for yet another and more important period of change.

The revitalization of downtown Haverhill became fashionable and breathed new life into the city. In October 1976, the Washington Street Shoe District was placed on the National Register of Historic Places.

No longer ignoring the needs of industry and no longer mystified by the intrusion of Interstate 495 in its backyard, the city has stopped yearning for a return to the days of the shoe industry and has begun to deal seriously with the problems of the present and the future. The city government, businesses, and the community have begun to lay the groundwork for an effective partnership that will lead to balanced economic growth, restoration of the city's architectural beauty, and renewal of its cultural and social heritage.

This book is about Haverhill's durable past and the continuities we have found amid change. It describes the patterns of life among the well known and the not-so-famous who have farmed the land, made the shoes, written the poetry, and programmed the computers. We have tried to recapture some of the rhythms of everyday life, the impetus of change, the ties of the past, and those indefinable factors that have shaped Haverhill's identity in its 350th year.

William Ellery Channing once wrote, "I sing New England, as she lights her fire/In every Prairie's Mind . . ." We sing in praise of Haverhill, a city that has contributed much to this nation's, and this region's, success.

In memory of James J. O'Malley (1933-1977), who loved his adopted city, and for Kathy, Terry, and Patsy, who have learned more about their hometown than they ever thought possible.

In memory of Serafino R. Tedesco (1896-1949), Haverhill shoeman, and Weaver Owen Tedesco (1924-1939), a son of Haverhill.

ACKNOWLEDGMENTS

The authors wish to extend special thanks to the following for their support: Ann F. Powell, Vice-President for College Relations, Bradford College; Howard W. Curtis, Librarian, the Haverhill Public Library; Museum of American Textile History, North Andover; we also wish to thank Bradford College for several Faculty Development Grants; "American Urban History," the National Endowment for the Humanities Seminar, Columbia University; Northeastern University for a sabbatical leave; the Newberry Library, Chicago, for an appointment as scholar-in-residence; Bernard J. "Barney" Gallagher, for years of caring; Julian Miller, for transcribing Isaac Merrill's diaries and Dennis Ford's letters; Kevin Trainor, for his encouragement; Eleanor Hollis Tedesco, for her support; and the Bradford College students whose research in Haverhill history provided us with invaluable resource materials, especially Todd Hamilton, Linda Huberdeau, Edward McKinney, Kathleen O'Malley, Steven Sardella, Deborah Day Smith, and Liz Barrett, Liz Bossi, Stephanie Dimock, Mark Mattoon, Robert Moran, Elizabeth Nash, and Deanna Yameen.

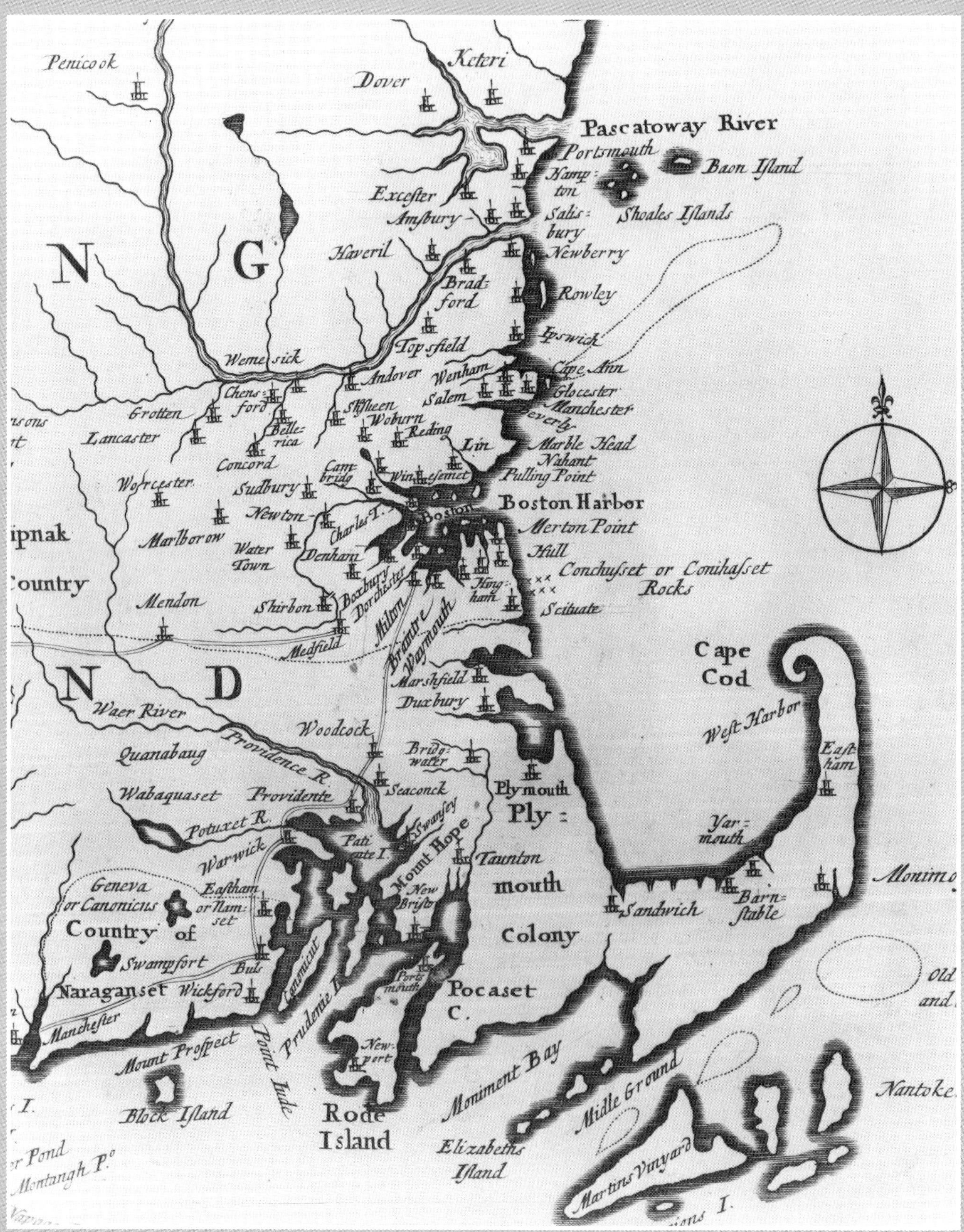

Penicook
Dover
Keteri
Pascatoway River
Portsmouth
Baon Island
Exceter
Hampton
Amsbury
Salisbury
Shoales Islands
Haveril
Newberry
Bradford
Rowley
Wemesick
Topsfield
Ipswich
Chensford
Andover
Wenham
Cape Ann
Grotten
Skuleen
Salem
Glocester
Manchester
Lancaster
Bellerica
Woburn
Reding
Beverly
Concord
Lin
Marble Head
Worcester
Cambridg
Winesemet
Nahant
Sudbury
Pulling Point
Newton
Charles T.
Boston Harbor
Marlborow
Boston
Merton Point
Water Town
Denham
Hull
Country
Mendon
Shirbon
Boxbury
Dorchester
Conchusset or Conihasset Rocks
Milton
Hingham
Medfeld
Braintre
Waymouth
Scituate
Waer River
Marshfield
Cape Cod
Quanabaug
Duxbury
West Harbor
Wabaquaset
Woodcock
Eastham
Providence R.
Bridgwater
Provident
Potuxet R.
Seaconck
Plymouth
Yarmouth
Warwick
Patience I.
Swansey
Ply:
Geneva or Canonicus
Eastham or Namset
Mount Hope
Taunton
Monimo
Country of
New Bristol
mouth
Sandwich
Barnstable
Swampfort
Buls
Colony
Naraganset
Wickford
Canonicut
Portsmouth
Pocaset C.
Manchester
Prudence I.
Mount Prospect
Point Iude
New port
Moniment Bay
Old and
Block Island
Rode Island
Middle Ground
Nantoke
Pond
Montangh Po
Elizabeths Island
Martins Vinyard
sons I.
N G N D

CHAPTER ONE

THE FRONTIER VILLAGE

Haverhill stretches along a jagged horizontal line in northeastern Massachusetts. Its form is shaped by the Merrimack River, which flows 12 miles along the city's boundary and through its center. The river's sinuous curves follow a southwesterly, now northwesterly, line, and then flow back to the southwest. Once Haverhill extended along the river for a dozen more miles, but eighteenth-century population dispersal and the desire for separate rule created the city's present western boundary. Colonial governments ordered the establishment of the curiously shaped northern boundary that parallels the river's twists and turns.

Many themes in the city's history can be traced to this elongated zigzag. The search for meadows and fresh water exerted a centrifugal pull away from the city's center. Clusters of families settled in the farthest eastern, northeastern, northern, and western corners of the township. As a result, the North Parish flows over into Plaistow, New Hampshire; Ayers Village overlaps both Methuen and Salem, New Hampshire; and Rocks Village blends imperceptibly with Merrimacport.

This quartering of the land has left its mark. Thus, Haverhill has two tales—one of its center, the other of its

A section of the map of New England used by Cotton Mather in his 1702 history shows the English settlements in the area at that time. Included are "Haverhill" and Bradford, which were on opposite sides of the Merrimack River, some 32 miles north of Boston and 16 miles upriver from the Atlantic Ocean. Courtesy, Trustees of the Haverhill Public Library

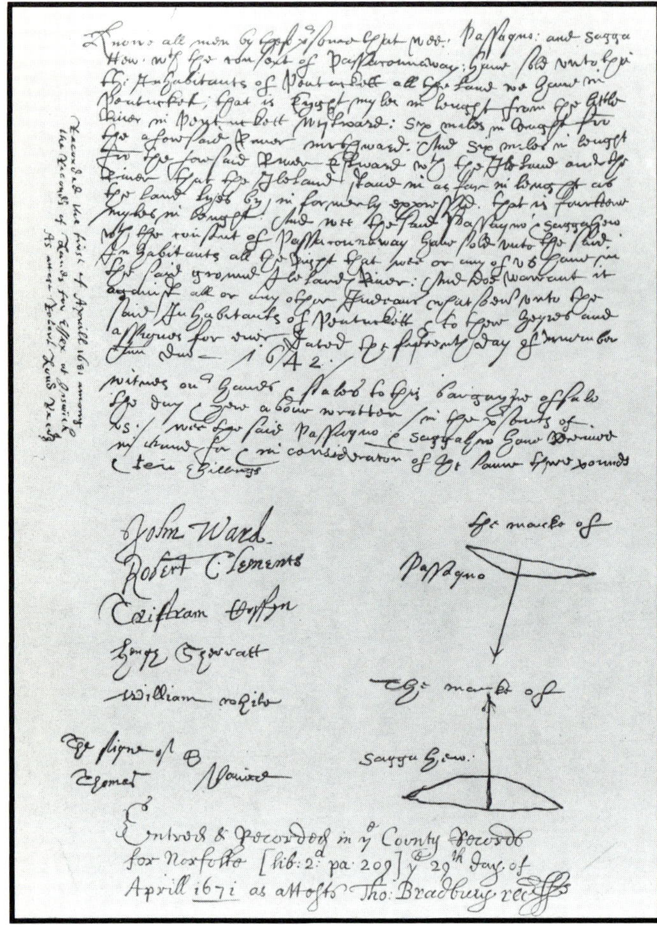

Above: *Shown here is a facsimile of the original deed between the English settlers and the few remaining Indians who laid claim to Pentucket. It was signed on November 15, 1642, by six of the settlers, as well as the Indians Passaquo and Saggahew, with the consent of Passaconnaway. The original deed is now at the Haverhill Historical Society.*

Facing page: *This fanciful mural, painted in the 1930s by Prescott Baston in the front hallway at Haverhill High School, depicts the site of the first settlement where the Mill Stream flowed into the Merrimack River. It may represent the arrival of John Ward, the settlement's first pastor, in 1641. Photo by Donald C. Freeman. Courtesy, Trustees of the Haverhill Public Library*

parishes and the settlements on the periphery. The former has been the political, mercantile, and industrial heart; the latter remained rural, separated by distance and interests from the center. The differences were heightened at the end of the nineteenth century when the downtown area became a mix of ethnic groups and religious interests while the outer areas remained Yankee and mainline Protestant.

Topography has also shaped Haverhill's history. The rolling terrain is dotted with rounded hills, the highest averaging just over 300 feet. The hills are strung along the Merrimack River, at the eastern end of town, and form a semicircular ring around the downtown area. Between the hills lie the long, narrow valleys carrying the creeks and rivers that promised meadows, fish, and waterpower to early settlers.

Nestled among the highest of Haverhill's hills are a trio of freshwater lakes—Kenoza, Saltonstall, and Round Pond—that probably dictated the siting of the first settlement immediately to the south. Directly across the river is Chadwick's Pond. All four bodies of water are relics of the receding glaciers from millenia ago. A fifth lake, Crystal, in Haverhill's northwestern corner, shares a similar interrelationship with a series of ponds across the state line in New Hampshire.

Only the northwestern quarter of the city, known as Ayers Village, has a generally flat topography. This West Meadow land was the first to draw settlers away from the original colonial site.

The terrain on which Haverhill would rise was shaped by nature and by its early inhabitants, the Pawtucket Indians, who called the area Pentucket. The well-watered meadows, the river, and the lakes provided the essential ingredients for farming. The sharp bend in the Merrimack at Ward Hill Neck offered an ideal fishing spot. The oceanside, with its shellfish and saltwater fish, was only half a day's walk to the east.

We have almost no historical record of these original inhabitants, save for a few symbols on an English treaty or an occasional court case involving a colonial innkeeper accused of serving liquor to an Indian. Hundreds of artifacts found in the area have enabled us not only to re-create their past but also to envision the landscape the first English settlers encountered.

Earlier historians loved to talk of dark, impene-
trable forests and virgin woods through which our
dauntless ancestors hacked openings and cleared
settlements. In reality, it is far more likely that the
colonists followed pathways through open, park-
like woods. The Indians regularly burned the under-
growth in wooded areas, resulting in a forest of
widely spaced trees with few shrubs.

Grass and tree-burning and farming were the duties of the women, while the men were hunters and
fishers. To the English, who saw hunting and fishing
as prerogatives of the leisure class, Indian women
appeared overworked and the men seemed lazy. The
English did not realize that this division of labor was
equal and well-adapted to the Indians' survival; in
fact, the Indian women's possession of all domestic
tools and accoutrements gave them sole authority
to decide when and where to move the settlement.

The white men who came to the Indian villages
at Pentucket may have found few, if any, inhabitants. European diseases (especially, it is now
thought, chicken pox) had already ravaged the native population. Though deserted, the land reflected
centuries of habitation. By 1640 the wooded areas
were probably still relatively easy to traverse. The
existing farmland would have given way to the first
pines and birches to invade such areas, and meadows would have begun to show the first encroach-
ment of red maples, alders, and willows. If the
settlers arrived in summer, they would have found
an abundance of berries in the abandoned fields.
Patches of rich, black soil would have indicated
where beaver ponds had once been.

For the English newcomers, the prospects were
promising but transitory. The Indians had survived
because they remained mobile, seeking out the most
fertile soil and the favored feeding ground. The colonists never understood this, and their lack of appreciation led them to view the Indian as an "ignorant
savage," whose elimination constituted "progress."

If the colonists' crops failed and their animals disappeared, that would be interpreted as a sign of God's will rather than English incompetence.

The English had different goals for the land. They believed in personal, not communal, property—the need to mark, bind, and legally register claims to land and establish stability through permanence. The colonists would mark their property with stakes, posts, and rails. This area was to be a "new" England that mirrored the old in appearance.

The Indians hunted animals but did not raise them. For the white man, dairy products were a basic part of the diet and wool was an essential mate-rial. Each required the maintenance of herds. The oxen and horses that the colonists had brought had to be watched and fed in winter. Pasture land and hay meadows were a necessity unknown to the Indians. Animal husbandry changed the land's appearance. Endless miles of fences within a property became the most visible sign of an Englishman's "improved" landscape.

The third difference between Indian and English views of the land concerned the products of their husbandry. The Indians lived at subsistence level, harvesting and hunting just enough for group survival. The English came from a society where the marketplace had been an influence on agriculture for at least three centuries. Land and property, and the products therefrom, were all commodities that could be traded for other goods or money or used as security for loans. If this attitude led to deforestation or overgrazing, that was "improvement" to the English.

The Puritan leadership that guided the colonists to New England had not intended to bring forth such attitudes. The constant search for fortune was to have been left behind in England. New England was to be the model of the new, reformed society. Settlements such as Haverhill were to be closed, corporate, and Christian communities, where church and town were one, where all worked together for the common good, and where deviation from the norm was to be discouraged.

When Nathaniel Ward of Ipswich and a number of Newbury men received permission from the Massachusetts General Court in 1640 to establish a new settlement, their intention was to replicate the pattern already in place in their respective towns. Selected families would live a structured life inspired by Puritan ideology.

How successfully intention translated into reality can be seen in the first century of Haverhill's story, which is best told along with the tale of its nearest neighbor, the community of Bradford. These twin towns, separated by the Merrimack River for 250 years, were joined as one in 1897.

Bradford had its beginnings as part of Rowley, established in the fall of 1639. Only one year separated the settling of Rowley and Pentucket—later renamed Haverhill—but their subsequent histories were quite different. Rowley began with 59 families, built around a core of 20 from Yorkshire who had emigrated with their pastor, the Reverend Ezekiel Rogers.

Haverhill had no such organized beginning. Few of its early inhabitants had families. Of the 12 men assumed to be the original settlers, at least five were not married until late in the 1640s and were probably young servants during the first years. Only two of the men, Henry Palmer and James Davis, had grown children to assist in the labors. Not until 1660 did Haverhill's population approach what Rowley had in 1639. Haverhill was never as unified a community. Rather, the town was an area of land specu-

Facing page and above: *John Ward's grandfather, also named John, served as pastor of the church of St. Mary's Parish of Haverhill, England, pictured here, for 25 years. Courtesy, Trustees of the Haverhill Public Library*

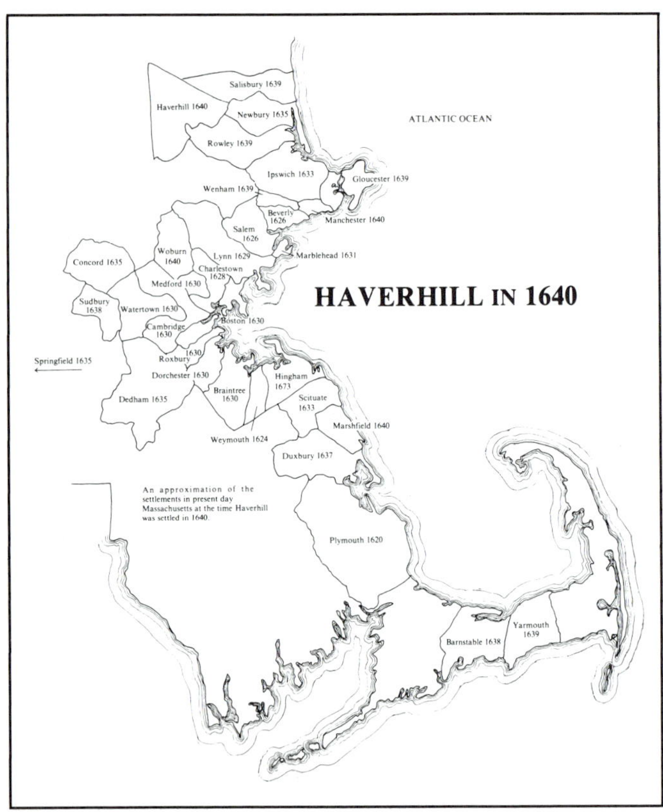

Above: In the period between the landing of the Pilgrims at Plymouth in 1620 and the arrival of the first English settlers in Haverhill in 1640, 33 permanent settlements were established within the boundaries of present-day Massachusetts. Haverhill was supposedly the thirtieth. Today the land claimed by these original settlements includes about 101 cities and towns in Massachusetts and New Hampshire. Map made by Susan E. Libby. Courtesy, Trustees of the Haverhill Public Library

Facing page: On March 3, 1648, Haverhill's citizens voted to erect a meetinghouse, 26 feet long by 20 feet wide. Built on Water Street near the first settlement, it probably stood in the present-day Pentucket Cemetery. Fred W. West drew this conjectural rendering of the structure in 1895. Courtesy, Trustees of the Haverhill Public Library

lation for such proprietors as Christopher Hussey of Salisbury and Joseph Jewett of Rowley, who held property in a number of communities and apparently did not live in Haverhill.

Haverhill also could not equal Rowley in the personality of the latter's religious leader. Ezekiel Rogers was the heart of Rowley's community even before the migration from England. A remarkably strong-willed man, he was prepared to take on Governor John Winthrop and the General Court to meet his demands for his community. In religion he was single-minded to the point of intolerance, and unforgiving of disagreement. According to Rowley folklore, when a stranger came to town and asked Rogers, "Are you the man that serves here?" the minister replied, "Serves here? I rule here!"

John Ward, Haverhill's religious leader, was Rogers' opposite, seldom mentioned in town, county, and colony records. The discerning Cotton Mather described Ward as having a "modest and bashful disposition, and very sparing of speaking, especially before strangers, or such as he thought his betters . . . he did not love to appear upon the public stage himself . . . he would never manage any ecclesiastical affairs in his church without previous and prudent consultations with the best advisors he knew."

A subdued Puritan minister was a rarity. In Haverhill, because of the congregational nature of the church, this meant that leadership devolved into the hands of laymen, a core of early arrivals whose robust health and extraordinary longevity gave them a lock on positions of power. By 1675, fully 35 years after the first settlement, 34 of 50 male heads of permanent families were still alive. The women fared better. Only 5 wives had died by 1665, and only 11 by 1675. Surprisingly, only 3 of the first 50 wives in the town are thought to have died after childbirth.

John Ward's "best advisors" were clearly Henry Palmer, William White, James and Thomas Davis, George Brown, and Nathaniel Saltonstall, Ward's Harvard-educated son-in-law. All were frequently recorded as selectmen, representatives, jurors, and magistrates. They wrote and witnessed wills and were invariably called upon to evaluate estate inventories. As staunch Puritans, they held a strong belief in predestination and in their conversion experience; these points are emphasized in the elaborate introductions to their wills.

I, James Davis . . . knowing assuredly that all men are mortal and that young men may die suddenly and old men must die, and how suddenly my own time may be in these desolate times, wherein the enemy seeks the destruction of our New England Israel, being through grace and the merits of my Lord and Saviour Jesus Christ in good hope of my eternal being in happiness, to whom I commit my soul, do hereby . . . settle my outward estate, which God in mercy hath hitherunto lent me . . .

In contrast to Haverhill's long-lived, modest minister and strong lay leadership, Rowley lost almost all of its prominent founding fathers by 1660. Ezekiel Rogers and a dozen of the most important men in that town had either died or moved away before the town was 25 years old. Rowley underwent two decades of endless squabbles, and the large land grant broke into smaller units. The westernmost end seceded in the 1660s and became incorporated as Bradford in the 1670s.

Haverhill's growth was slow but steady. Its isolation spared it from many of the epidemic diseases that spread through the coastal communities, and wide spacing of house sites controlled incidences of cholera, typhoid and other diseases resulting from overcrowding.

However, death had other means of claiming victims. Death by accident was as likely a killer of young adults as was disease. "Benjamin, son of Will. Hutchins, was killed by a sled going over him" (Bradford Town Records, April 4, 1676). Also, during the last 25 years of the seventeenth century, the town lived under the threat of attack by Indian allies of the French. An entire generation, born in the 1670s, grew to adulthood, married, and raised families while haunted by the possibility that they might share their neighbors' fates of kidnapping and murder. The most tragic Indian raid occurred on "Bloody Sunday," August 28, 1708. Sixteen people were killed, including minister Benjamin Rolfe, merchant Simon Wainwright, and Captain Samuel Ayer.

Haverhill's most familiar story is that of Hannah Duston, who was taken prisoner during a 1697 attack that left 40 dead, including her one-week-old

child. She escaped and took her vengeance, returning to Haverhill with the scalps of her captors. Recent scholarship has raised questions about this grisly action, but the power of legend remains strong, and Hannah Duston is the only individual local celebrity for whom a public sculpture has been erected.

The sensationalism of the Indian menace hides the ordinariness of life in this era. Though there are few physical remains from Haverhill's first century, careful searching in the records illuminates the everyday life of the pioneers and adds a third dimension to their memories. A contract between John Whittier, carpenter, and Robert Swan describes the 1680s construction of a house:

The frame [is] to be eight and forty feet long, twenty feet wide, with thirteen foot and a half between joints, the ends and sides to be clapboarded excepting that part which will be between the old house, and that the roof to be covered with boards and short shingles, to make nine window frames, and two pair of casement frames, to lay six floors, to make four partitions joining to the 'chimles' or near to them, to make one outside door and five other doors, and to make three pairs of stairs, and the said John to cut the timbers upon the said Robert's right either of land or common.

According to the contract, Whittier was to be paid for his work in corn, oats, "good, sound, neat cattle to be fat and fit for the slaughter, bulls excepted," and 20 shillings. Swan was to allow four shillings per week for the workmen's food.

The furnishings of such a home could be as simple as those listed in Joseph Heath's 1673 inventory— "clothes, boots, shoes, three hats, linen, and ribbon; two saddles, arms, and a pillion; a cutlass and a case of pistols and holster; 21 pounds of cotton and a bed mat; four trays, churns, and other wooden ware; one iron pot and pot hooks, two porringers, and a pewter platter."

In contrast, the inventory of widow Sarah Gage's estate listed room after room of belongings, including a "red petticoat [and] another red petticoat."

The estate left by the Reverend Benjamin Rolfe suggests a sophistication leagues removed from the earlier generation's way of life. The listing of the Rolfe household goods included an extensive library (valued at £14), pewter so plentiful it had to be evaluated by weight (6 platters weighing 47 pounds, 17 plates, 5 old platters weighing 13 pounds), and eleven turkish-worked chairs and two turkish-worked carpets—an exotic touch in that frontier community.

At the end of the inventory were reminders of a more dangerous world: the "old tubs, an old chest and meal troughs, and three broken trunks" among which Rolfe's slave, Hagar, concealed and saved two of his children during the Bloody Sunday attack.

Public records can give us a sense of seventeenth century colonial life, which was occasionally spiced with scandal. For example, Mary Pearson of Bradford was called to testify in a paternity case concerning Sarah Savery and John Carrell, an Irish servant in the Pearson house.

She noticed many uncivil carriages between them and (Mary) reproved Sarah for it, but she answered that she loved him, and she believed he loved her, for he intended to ask her father for her, and she thought her father would be willing. Carrell said that Sarah would lay 'the trouble' to [Caleb] Hopkinson, for he himself was a poor fellow who could not maintain her, and he would run away if he thought she would lay it [her pregnancy] to him (Essex County Quarterly Court, 1685).

Robert Swan carried on a lifelong battle against authority. In the following February 1686 incident, he complained about being taxed, or rated, for more property than he had declared.

You have rated devilishly and unrighteously.

And Josiah Gage made answer that, so far as he knew, they had rated according as people gave in and so far as they knew what people had rateable for. Said Gage to Swan,
You withheld one yoke of oxen, but we knowing it,

we rated you for them.

Why, said Swan, I had two oxen.

But, said Daniel Ladd, you had four oxen!

But, said Swan to Ladd, you lie.

But, said Ladd to Swan, you lie, and I can prove it.

And, said Gage, I can testify that you had four oxen, Goodman Swan, at the time of assessment.

Swan said, no, I had not.

Then, Ladd replied to Swan, had you but only Black and Goldie, the old oxen?

Then Swan said he had none but them, and yet afterward Swan said that he did believe that he gave in four oxen (Essex County Quarterly Court, 1686).

Swan went on to say that "men were led about by the laws like a company of puppy-dogs." He was constantly involved in land deals, in fights over town and church rates, and in arguments over contracts. His sons were brawlers and his sons-in-law were charged with fathering illegitimate children. But his presence could be tolerated, for each of his property moves took him and his family further away from the town center.

A positive side of frontier life was the freedom such a location provided. Haverhill's size and isolation provided a safety valve for troublemakers. A person like Robert Swan could be a volatile irritant in a socially and geographically confined space. The same person in a place the size of Haverhill could be pushed on westward beyond the Spicket River lands, or north past any open land. In 1725, when the westernmost part of Haverhill seceded to form the new town of Methuen, its leaders included numerous Swans who were grandsons and true attitudinal heirs of old Robert.

The original town center would remain the domain of the powerful and of the obedient. The more independent spirits would move to the periphery, and by Haverhill's 100th anniversary in 1740, that meant land beyond the town's borders.

ELIZABETH WARD SALTONSTALL

After her teenage daughter left for Cambridge to visit relatives, a mother in Haverhill wrote to her daughter on May 26, 1684, in a vexed tone:

Look among the things you carried with you whither you did not carry that shift which I ordered you to leave behind you. I can not find it at home. If you have it, send it by Goodman West or send me word where you left it. . . Work is now hard upon us and help small. Betsey Warner [a household servant] was sent for home a few days after you went. Her father and others of the family being sick . . . I cannot enlarge at present [i.e., on the difficulties at home] being much straightened of time but only a strict charge upon you that you will endeavor so to walk that you may not dishonor God nor scandalize religion nor grieve the hearts of dear parents and friends who wish you as well as their own souls.

The words belonged to Elizabeth Ward Saltonstall, the daughter of

Haverhill's revered first minister, John Ward. Through her marriage to Nathaniel Saltonstall, Elizabeth became connected to one of the few families in Colonial Massachusetts who had ties to England's landed gentry. Nathaniel's father, Sir Richard, was a founder of the Massachusetts Bay Company. His stature gave Nathaniel access to numerous legislative, judicial, and military positions.

From a house facing the Merrimack River, the Saltonstalls created a dynasty that endured in Haverhill until the twentieth century and provided generations of respected leaders.

The letters from Elizabeth and Nathaniel to their teenage daughter, also named Elizabeth, remind us that the Saltonstalls were an ordinary family despite their name and prestige.

Loving Daughter, I have sent by Marten Ford your brothers' stockings. Pray let them be well dried before they wear them . . . Rich. and Natt are gone to . . . their own errands. We want them for many things especially to read to your Grand [father Ward] . . . Send me some mustard by Marten Ford, our old store is almost gone. (December 6, 1688)

(From Nathaniel) We are so surrounded with news of depredations, and losses of lives [from Indian attacks to the north] . . . that the people of this place are gone into Garrisons, on which account our place or garrison is stuffed full with lodgers . . . We are generally in health tho in heaps, for every place

is taken with beds and with people. (July 31, 1694)

[I]t's our duty . . . to return an answer before now but I beg that the . . . disturbances we are under by reason of ould Jersey [the family cow] being billetted in the house besides about 60 garrison people and but little help may bespeak an excuse for me. (August 27, 1694)

Above: *The Saltonstall Seat was one of the most important homes ever built in Haverhill. Courtesy, Trustees of the Haverhill Public Library*

Left: *Gurdon Saltonstall, one of the four children of Nathaniel and Elizabeth Ward Saltonstall, served 16 years as the governor of Connecticut. Courtesy, Trustees of the Haverhill Public Library.*

The concern and caring reflected in the letters recall a humanity that history has tended to mythicize. Even martyrs had their domestic side, as we learn from the Saltonstalls' comment on two of their boarders, Benjamin Rolfe, successor to John Ward, and his new bride: "Mr. Rolfe and his wife are in his wonted chamber and, for all I see, love one another, for they are not up as soon as the sun."

CHAPTER TWO

The Mercantile Community

We beg your Excellencies and Honors will be pleased to have a tender regard to the Old Parish that was once the center of a very large town and is now become to be very small." So wrote Joshua Bayley and James Pearson of the committee for the old parish in Haverhill to the Massachusetts General Court, June 14, 1743. The letter was a response to a petition from inhabitants in the east end of Haverhill for a separate parish. The First Parish had good reason to object to the request, for during the previous 15 years the Methuen area had been lost to the town, and one-third of Haverhill's remaining population, territory, and property had been taken by the final determination of the New Hampshire borderline.

Measured solely in terms of the reduction in size and numbers, the 1740s could have been considered hard times for the town on the Merrimack. Yet in the long run the changes benefited the community. Political domination of the original, far-flung Haverhill carried a high cost; the smaller-sized Haverhill was much easier to govern, protect, educate, and enrich. Eighteenth-century Haverhill found it worthwhile to replace political domination with economic well-being.

Above: *The 340-ton ship* Ulysses, *of Salem, was built in a Haverhill shipyard in 1798. All types of sailing vessels were constructed along the Merrimack River in Haverhill and Bradford between 1690 and 1840, when the last one was launched. Shipbuilding was the main non-agricultural occupation in the area in the eighteenth century. Courtesy, Trustees of the Haverhill Public Library*

Facing page: *The East Meadow River was used for water power to operate mills as early as the 1690s. There was a sawmill and a gristmill near the Amesbury (now Merrimack) line begun by Joseph Peaslee in 1693; a woolen mill off Middle Road where John Chase manufactured cloth and carpets in the 1800s; a sawmill, gristmill, and fulling mill near the present outlet of Millvale Reservoir beginning in 1757; and the gristmill shown above, known as Johnson's Mill, begun by Thomas Johnson in the 1790s. This mill was later used by the Shattuck family, until the 1880s. Photo by Austin P. Nichols. Courtesy, Trustees of the Haverhill Public Library*

Agriculture was at a very low ebb in Massachusetts in the first half of the eighteenth century as a consequence of overuse of the soil. Population growth, combined with limited mobility in the last quarter of the seventeenth century, had slowed the process of opening up land, which in turn led to intensive use of the existing land. The agricultural revolution sweeping northwestern Europe was still 50 years away for New England.

Haverhill's northern lands, lost to New Hampshire, were at a stage where much labor was expended for little profit. A 1741 survey showed that the Massachusetts portion had one-and-a-half times the corn fields, twice the hay fields, three-and-a-half times the pasture, and five times the acreage in orchards per household. Hay and apples were cash crops that offered far greater return for far less effort than the grain crops that occupied up to half of the worked land to the north.

Haverhill's greatest profits, though, came not from its fields but from its location on the Merrimack River. That waterway was the primary route for valley trade until the advent of the railroad in the mid-nineteenth century. The new towns in the center of New Hampshire, such as Londonderry and Concord, required a market for the lumber and cattle they produced, and Haverhill was the most logical and accessible place.

Boats were built for commercial use as early as the 1670s. Court records describe the ketches and sloops contructed by carpenter John Haseltine and tanner Daniel Ela for both local and Boston captains. Imports from the West Indies (especially sugar for rum) and from England increased greatly during the eighteenth century; the waterside warehouses of the town were constantly filled with raw materials from the north country and finished goods from abroad.

The town was economically diversified by the mid-1700s. Agriculture became a part-time pursuit for the inhabitants of the center of town. Hired hands tended farms and animals while landowners pursued more lucrative occupations in trade, crafts, and the professions. This diversity began to attract a new population, one without ties to the original settlers, who brought new ideas and perspectives. Many of the names on the town records of the 1740s are Scotch-Irish in origin, including James Duncan, trader, and James McHard, distiller.

At the start of its second century, Haverhill had taken on a new personality. The original Puritan ideal of community and control had been physically broken by territorial losses and the creation of separate parishes to the north (1730), west (1734), and east (1743) of the town.

Religious uniformity also disappeared. Traditional theology and religious practices were undermined by the revivalist movement known as the Great Awakening. Direct outcomes of this movement were the challenge to ministerial authority in the 1750s in the West Parish led by Joseph Haynes and the establishment of a Baptist society under Hezekiah Smith in the First Parish in 1765.

Profits had become a more tangible reward than salvation. Young Leverett Saltonstall, fresh from Harvard College, lamented in 1807 that "no people on earth have so little local and I may say family attachment as the New Englander. They know and feel but little love for anything but gold. 'O give me gold ye Gods' is their universal prayer."

The original Puritan hope for a closed, cooperative community had an inherent flaw, for no town could limit itself completely to church members in full communion—"the visible saints." Intermarriage, migrations, and community needs all opened the town to "non-saints." Rather than undergo the scrutiny of proving a conversion experience, which was necessary for acceptance into the select membership of the church, it was easier to become a freeman and take part in town affairs. Disagreements grew between town and church, usually over ministerial pay and church buildings and repairs.

Haverhill did have an alternative way to try to maintain a select group in power. The members of this group were the "proprietors," or commoners, who by right of inheritance from the early settlers controlled gifts and sales of all undivided land, including any land used as "commons" in any part of the town's original grant. There was an ongoing conflict in the town's first hundred years between commoners and the noncommoners who had to buy their property from the proprietors. Proprietors invariably had the law on their side, while noncommoners had strength in numbers and could usually sway town elections to balance the power of the elite.

These proprietors reflected an old England where landowners were considered the natural leaders of society and of all other institutions of power. Haverhill's noncommoners represented a newer school of thought, an egalitarian view emphasizing that salvation was not necessarily reflected in social status and that authority rested in the community.

Economic change in Haverhill added a new dimension to this community split. The leading proprietors, including John White, Richard Hazen, and Judge Richard Saltonstall, resided in the First Parish, the old center of town. The more democratic elements tended to live in the outlying districts, especially the West Parish where a particularly vocal group was ensconced. The proprietors drew support from the mercantile newcomers, who lived in the center and received land there for the wharves, mills, distilleries, and stores that were turning the village into a commercial magnet.

With the collapse of the Puritan communal ideal, patriotism took on a more important role in holding the community together. Although three generations separated the colonists from England, by the middle of the eighteenth century the great-grandchildren of the pioneers were drawn back into the circle of England's influence and power. The re-Anglicization of American culture meant that,

on the eve of the Revolution of 1776, Americans were more English than they had been since the first years of settlement. The renewed ties were reflected in architecture, furniture, dress, and especially ideas.

England had become a world power since the days of the Pilgrims, and Americans took enormous pride in their kinship. That patriotism showed in the colonists' response to the French and Indian Wars. No earlier generation would so willingly have undertaken the siege of Louisbourg in Nova Scotia in 1745; Haverhill men were there, as well as at Crown Point and Ticonderoga in New York in 1759. Haverhill volunteers came from all levels of society, from Captain Edmund Mooers, Esquire, to his servant, "Negro Jack."

Renewed contact with England also brought the colonists into touch with the revolutionary political theories of that country, and when the relationship between mother country and colonies became strained in the 1770s, the colonies demonstrated how well they had learned their lessons, using England's own ideas to justify rebellion and revolution. As tensions increased between England and the American colonies, the newfound patriotism of the 1750s did not disappear but was transferred from Britain to America.

For Haverhill, patriotism provided not only a new bond and a new sense of belonging but also meant a victory for democratic change. Patriotism was not measured by economic or social status, only by enthusiasm. The success of the democratic movement was clearly seen in late September 1774, when men from the combined Committees of Correspondence of Haverhill and Bradford, led by Thomas Eaton of the West Parish, James Duncan of the village, and Peter Russell of Bradford, descended on the sheriff of Essex County, Colonel Richard Saltonstall, at his "small paternal estate" on Water Street.

Saltonstall, the fourth generation of that distinguished Haverhill family and a hero during the French and Indian War, was driven from town for his Tory sentiments. In a 1777 request to the British government for compensation for his personal and professional losses, Saltonstall described the "outrageous and lawless violence of the populace" and the "mortifying necessity . . . of leaving his estate and effects to the ravages of a licentious popu-

lace." He professed himself "not conscious of having wantonly provoked the resentments of his deluded countrymen."

Haverhill and Bradford forged strong chains of local and regional unity in the rebellion. Both towns contributed money and goods to further the struggle. Heroes ranged from Lieutenant Colonel (later General) James Brickett, a surgeon who fought next to Colonel William Prescott at Bunker Hill, and Ensign James Walker, who was at the capture of Trenton, to fifteen-year-olds Thomas Page and Nathaniel Clark, fifer and drummer, respectively, during the last years of the war. Also involved were those on the home front, such as the widow Prudence Carlton, who loaned £60 to the town of Haverhill to help with expenses, and Jeremiah Haseltine of the East Parish, who collected "9 shirts, 7 pr. shoes, & 10 pr. stockens" during a clothing drive for the army.

Unity, however, was short-lived. The conflicts latent in the town's structure resurfaced after peace and independence had been established. Disagreements over governmental power divided the town into Federalists and Democratic-Republicans.

A section of Mrs. Green's print of downtown Haverhill, circa 1814, showing the Kendrick (later Caldwell) shipyard, the Baptist church at the corner of Merrimack and Pecker streets, and the Saltonstall mansion behind a fence and two trees. Courtesy, Trustees of the Haverhill Public Library

Economic differences between farmers and traders intensified in the postwar turmoil. A clear stylistic separation emerged between the cosmopolitan Georgian society in the town and the frugal, Yankee life in the rural parishes. The resulting tension may well have been the means by which Haverhill progressed. With neither group in clear domination, the continuing struggle led to periods of progress followed by long spells of resistance.

Haverhill captured the results of its progress in an 1814 sketch by an artist identified only as Mrs. Green. The village is shown from Mill Street on the east to the Little River on the west. A continuous row of buildings stretches along the river and on Main Street up to the First Parish church. The large Baptist church looms behind a row of small cottages on Merrimack Street. Though George Washington called it the "pleasantest village I have passed through" on his 1789 visit, Leverett Saltonstall in his 1815 *Historical Sketch* admitted that "Haverhill is not so handsome . . . as its local situation deserves . . . The river or water street is too narrow and too near the bank. The number of ordinary buildings on the lower side of the street interrupts the view from the houses, and injures the appearance of the town from the opposite shore." He suggested that "a road parallel to the river . . . on the brow of the hill . . . commanding a most extensive prospect," would help.

Twenty-five years earlier, Saltonstall's father, Dr. Nathaniel Saltonstall, had built the then-grandest house in town on Merrimack Street. It had been sited to allow an unrestricted view from its front windows, over its terraced lawns, to the river. By the time Mrs. Green sketched the town, the Saltonstall mansion had been crowded in by new houses and shops. Clusters of multi-level brick buildings stood a few doors to the east at White's Corner, the terminus of the new Haverhill bridge, a three-arched engineering marvel built in 1794. The bridge increased overland trade and drew Haverhill further into the Boston market.

There were more than 30 shops in Haverhill by 1815 and while shipbuilding was still a viable business employing 50 to 60 men per year, Haverhill was undergoing big economic changes through the growing world of manufacture. Profit-minded citizens took advantage of the immense number of cattle that reached the town for the cattle market. If there was a profit to be made in trading the animals wholesale, even more could be made from processing them for retail sale. This realization gave rise to a new economy. Salt beef was shipped downriver in casks for export. The East Parish developed the production of combs from horns. Leather from the tanners along Mill Creek became gloves and plaited ware for saddles, harnesses, and carriages. And, as a portent of the future, the first signs of an organized shoe industry appeared.

Samuel Varnum, a local lawyer, reported to his brother-in-law Leverett Saltonstall in 1811 that more than 20,000 pairs of shoes had been sent from the town that year, 15,000 from entrepreneurs Warner Whittier and James Atwood alone. Within 20 years the number of shoes shipped from town skyrocketed to 1,500,000 pairs annually.

Expansion at this rate spelled the end of the Georgian town, the eventual disappearance of those picturesque buildings that are idealized as typical of New England—white clapboard houses, taverns on the green, and an austere Congregational church in the center of town. Nostalgia was not profitable in the nineteenth century. Georgian mansions yielded to utilitarian brick blocks. Then, with the arrival of the railroad in the 1830s, Haverhill's growth was more securely tied to the downtown area.

That first age of elegance has disappeared from downtown Haverhill. The houses and gardens, the terraces on the river, the small, select world of comfortable people have all vanished. A rural version of the architecture can be found at Rocks Village, a reminder that industrial growth bypassed the East Parish.

Timothy Dwight, president of Yale and an inveterate traveler and commentator on New England, passed through the area about 1812. He commented:

The houses are generally good, and some of them are handsome ... The manners of the inhabitants in general are very civil and becoming. Those of the most respectable people are plain, frank, easy, and unaffected. The gentlemen and ladies are well bred and intelligent, and recommend themselves not a little to the esteem and attachment of a traveler. We saw at church a numerous congregation, well-dressed, decorous, and reverential in their deportment.

Twenty-three-year-old Elizabeth Cranch, visiting the family of merchant John White in their mansion on Water Street, recorded in her diary on January 18, 1786, "Just at sunset the prospect from my chamber window most enchantingly beautiful— the river perfectly calm—the western sky just tinged with that rich and lovely coloring which art can never imitate." The diary is filled with descriptions of visits, tea parties, formal balls, and sleigh rides downriver. One of her companions was her young cousin, John Quincy Adams, who was residing with his aunt and uncle, the Reverend John Shaw, pastor of the First Parish. These two Boston-area visitors found Haverhill society far from rustic.

Twenty years after Elizabeth Cranch wrote in her diary, Anna Saltonstall received a letter from her older brother, Leverett, who advised her:

Now we shall have some pleasant weather. Let it not pass unimproved by you in rural walks. Stroll along the banks of the charming Merrimack; vary your walks to the ponds ... Nature has been peculiarly bountiful to Haverhill in spreading around it a rich scenery and not to enjoy it is ingratitude.

How delightful, and what a far cry from the rigorous endurance of the old frontier village. At about the same time, Mary Orne Tucker wrote in her diary of a stroll on the Merrimack:

April 28 [1802] ... The weather was fine this morning and tempted us to stray—these morning walks are a great indulgence, and I believe they are healthful, but they sadly interrupt the business of the day, the mind gets so dissipated, it is no easy task to discharge the humble duties of domestic life, as my situation in life renders the discharge of such duties very important. I must be careful not too often to be tempted to such relaxations. I am not much in the habit of gadding.

The Puritan work ethic was creating a world of profit and luxury. At the same time, that ethic could still induce a twinge of guilt over the simple enjoyment of nature's loveliness.

THE KIMBALLS AND THEIR HOME

Houses, like families, have genealogies that often parallel the lives of their inhabitants. Rooms are added or removed, landscaping altered, paint and paper put on or taken off. Enough traces usually remain to guide the conscientious researcher back through a structure's generations.

The Kimball family came to Bradford in 1663. The impact of their presence is reflected in the abundance of people, houses, streets, and gravestones bearing the Kimball name. One branch of the family built a house in 1692 that faced the town common and remained in the family until 1921.

Bradford College bought the house in 1967 and restored it to its 1803 appearance. Upon removing the clapboards and baring the foundation, it was possible to see the genealogy of the house. Research into the shapes and styles of its paneling and fireplaces suggested how the house evolved in tandem with the family.

Benjamin Kimball, first of that name in Bradford, gave his son Richard six acres of land and £20 with which to build a house. Richard's house was a one-room cottage with a loft and was probably built in the summer of 1692.

To accommodate his growing family, Richard added a second

Above: *The Kimball Homestead on Salem Street, built by Richard Kimball in 1692, was used as a tavern from around 1765 until the time of the temperance movement in the 1830s. Courtesy, Trustees of the Haverhill Public Library*

Below: *In the early days stages such as the one shown probably stopped at Bradford Common by the Kimball Tavern. Courtesy, Trustees of the Haverhill Public Library*

room about 15 years later to the east of the first room, and a full second floor was finished. Much of the material was reused wood. The paneling and a large beam in the new east room suggest that a larger structure dating from the mid-to-late 1660s was the source of the wood. About the time that Kimball enlarged his house, Haverhill had suffered the Bloody Sunday attack that left a number of houses vacant. The parsonage, where Benjamin Rolfe had lived, was built in 1668 and could have been the source of the architectural pieces used in the Bradford house.

Richard's son, Stephen, inherited the property. He probably redid the parlor at the time of his marriage in 1736, for the paneling dates from that period.

In the next generation, the elder

son, Jacob, took over the house and added the Georgian-style front entry tower. Jacob converted the house into a tavern in 1765 by adding a tap room on the east end and raising the roof to accommodate more rooms. He and his sons, Jacob and Moses, who inherited the home from his brother, all held innkeeper's licenses. Since it faced the Common and the meeting house, the tavern became an ideal spot to conduct post-meeting business.

It was at that tavern that 30 local men met to found a private academy for Bradford girls and boys. Moses served as a trustee of the new Bradford Academy, sent his children there, and took in out-of-town students as boarders. In 1814 he had four boys and five girls boarding in his upstairs rooms, an early version of a coeducational dormitory.

Moses' son, also named Jacob, had two daughters who never married. To keep them properly employed, he purchased the old Bradford schoolhouse dating from 1761 and moved it to the northeastern corner of his own house, where the sisters kept a private school for years. They were the last Kimballs to occupy the house.

SEWING MACHINE WARE HOUSE
FLANDERS & Co.
TELEGRAPH
OFFICE

CHAPTER THREE

ISAAC MERRILL'S TOWN

Isaac Watts Merrill, 67 years of age, left his two-story brick house on Main Street in the North Parish of Haverhill early one December morning in 1870. A dusting of snow on the ground would soon melt under the midday sun. Merrill's destination was Daniel Harriman's shoe manufactory in downtown Haverhill, where he would leave a set of misses' shoes, receive his pay, and pick up cut stock for another set of 75 pairs of shoes. As usual, Merrill, a short, lame fellow, depended on a neighbor for transportation, for he had never owned a horse and carriage.

This was a busy season for the shoemaker and his friends. Earlier in the week they had participated in the re-election of Warner R. Whittier, Haverhill's first mayor under the new city charter. It was also the season for butchering hogs to provide meat for wintertime meals. At that time hogs were sold at 13 cents a pound, a much better bargain than the more expensive poultry featured in the markets for Thanksgiving, two weeks earlier. Turkeys cost up to 30 cents a pound, and chickens 28 cents a pound. Merrill would have to watch his expenses, for the shoe business was slow this year. Harriman was paying only 16 cents a pair to independent shoemakers like Merrill, so it

This December 1870 photograph, looking east toward White's Corner, depicts Merrimack Street. On the left is the cellar hole of the Saltonstall house, which was moved in November from here to Saltonstall Road overlooking Plug Pond. Shortly thereafter, the pond was renamed Lake Saltonstall in honor of the illustrious family. Courtesy, Trustees of the Haverhill Public Library

would take four days of work, making an average of five pairs a day, for Merrill to afford a small turkey.

On his journey into town, Merrill might have passed the time recalling similar trips 40 years earlier. His employer then was Daniel Hobson of Bradford. Ironically, the price paid for Merrill's work was higher then: 20-25 cents a pair. During that time Merrill specialized in French-edged men's boots; by 1870, ladies' shoes comprised the bulk of his work. In the 1830s, pork, turkey, eggs, and butter sold for half their 1870 prices.

The most visible contrast, however, was in Haverhill itself. Not far beyond Charles Duston's house, where Primrose Street ran into Main Street, the wagon carrying Merrill entered a town that could not have been envisioned in the 1830s. If the journey had followed Primrose Street, the course would run parallel to the Boston and Maine Railroad track, which carved a north-south line through the center of the town and into New Hampshire. The travelers would proceed through the heart of the Acre, the Irish enclave that had turned the open fields north of Winter Street into a rabbit warren of narrow streets and crowded buildings.

Merrill was an enthusiast for the railroad. A longtime shareholder, he kept close tabs on its construction through his neighborhood, and he traveled on its tracks all over the Northeast on business trips and vacations.

Merrill kept a diary, a priceless legacy containing 50 years of Haverhill history. From 1828 to 1878, he recorded an unparalleled study of the ordinary rhythms of everyday life: the weather; Sunday sermons; births, deaths, and marriages; and passersby who stopped to warm themselves, have a meal, exchange some gossip, or share a fiddle tune. He reminds us of the anguish when a neighbor's barn burns or a business fails; the pain over the death of a young bride, or the sudden illness of a promising scholar; the sorrow when an old friend becomes deranged and is taken to the state hospital in Worcester; the horror of a neighbor murdering a friend.

Merrill also described the seasonal rhythms to which residents of the outlying parishes still responded long after the downtown area had adjusted to factory bells and time clocks. On the periphery of the town, nature still controlled the calendar. Time was measured by the agricultural demands of plowing, planting, harvesting, and storing. In 1870

Above: *The Haverhill Bridge, a wooden toll-bridge between Haverhill and Bradford, was in use from 1794 until 1873 when it was replaced by an iron bridge. It was covered in 1825, as shown in this photograph taken during a spring "freshet," or flood, in the late 1860s. Courtesy, Trustees of the Haverhill Public Library*

Facing page, top: *The house of Isaac Merrill, at 73 Plaistow Road, looked like this around the time of his death in 1878. In the diary which he kept for 50 years, Merrill documented nearly everything that happened to the house from the time he broke ground for the cellar hole on August 12, 1830. His North Parish neighborhood, the shoemaking trade, and Haverhill's transition from an agricultural to an industrial city are all included in Isaac's chronicles. Courtesy, Trustees of the Haverhill Public Library*

Facing page, bottom: *The land west of Main Street at Duston Square was purchased in August 1697 by Thomas Duston with money appropriated by the Massachusetts General Court. Duston built this house, and his descendants lived in it until Dr. Thomas Duston built a new brick house circa 1810. The land finally went out of the Duston family in the 1870s. Courtesy, Trustees of the Haverhill Public Library*

Above and facing page: The General Court of the Commonwealth of Massachusetts passed legislation in 1830 that required every community to have a "correct survey of the town made." Many communities had these surveys printed as lithographs; these were Haverhill's and Bradford's first printed maps. In Bradford, every house was identified, and the town voted to provide a map for every household. In Haverhill, however, the map was sold by subscription, and only those homeowners who purchased a subscription had their houses identified. Courtesy, Trustees of the Haverhill Public Library

Merrill was still of this vanishing rural world. He made his shoes whenever he found time. If he chose to go haying or blueberrying, to spend a day or a week at Boars Head on Hampton Beach, or just ride around for a day with the fish peddler or the baker, he would do so. Conversely, if the weather was right and the light was good, and no one interrupted him, he might finish 10 pairs of shoes in one day—three days' work.

Merrill's interests were catholic and progressive. He read Voltaire, sang Handel and Haydn oratorios with the Sacred Music Society, subscribed to daily Boston newspapers, and took an active part in Whig and Republican party politics. Though he and his father, Moses Merrill, Esquire, stayed in their corner of the North Parish, his brothers, Gyles and Moses, Jr., were white-collar managers whose employment took them far from home, but never out of touch.

The world came to Merrill. He enjoyed visits from Irishmen, French-Canadians, Germans, and Italians, as well as a Dutchman who "stopped to mend

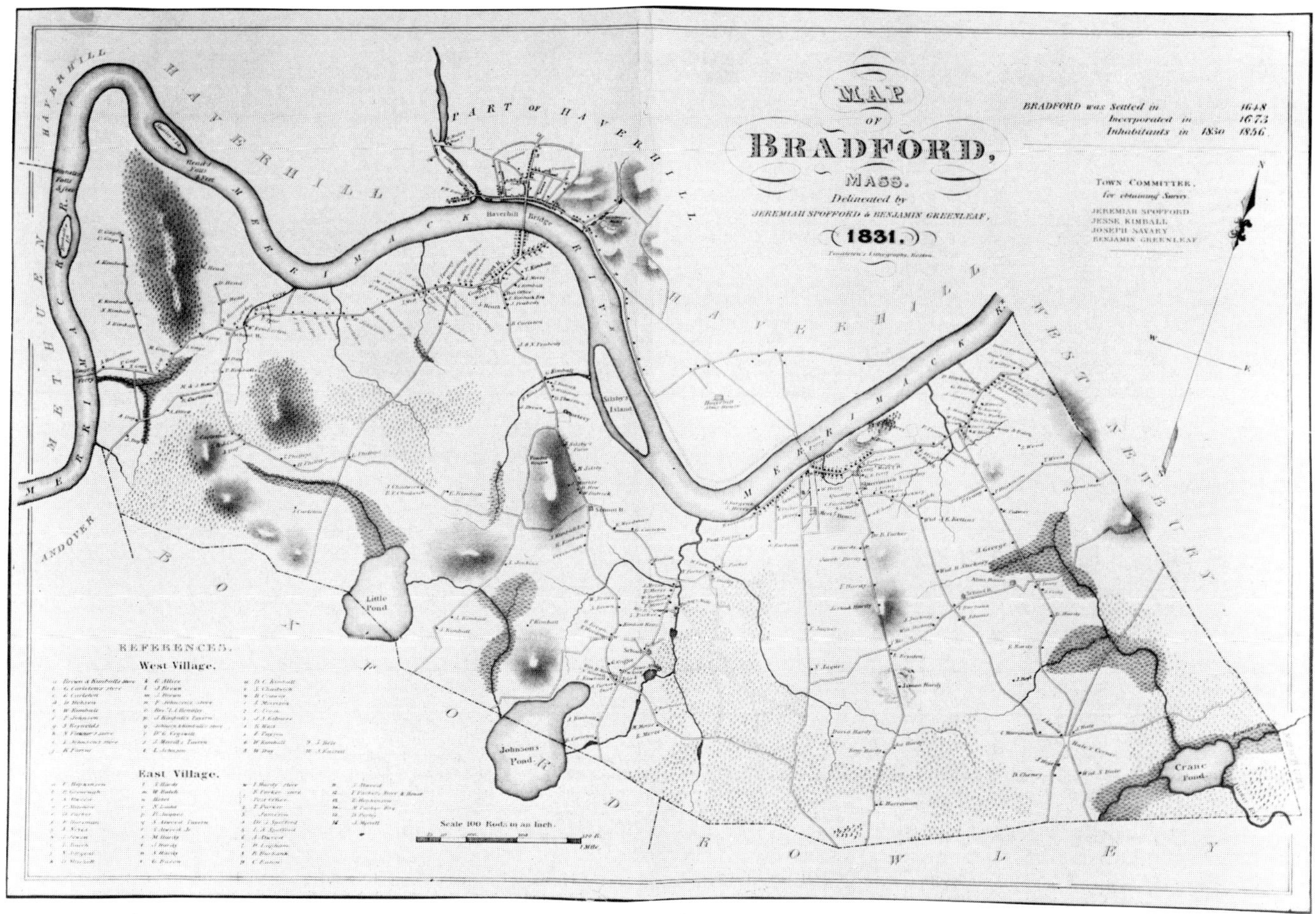

his pantaloons," a Turk sent to America by his parents during the Crimean War, runaway slaves from the South, and a young man from the island of Madeira who attended Bradford Academy and remained in the area—and once ran away with Merrill's wife for a few weeks! Without ever moving more than a few yards from his birthplace, Merrill kept in touch with a large network of neighbors and relatives who went to college, tried prospecting in California, taught in the post-Civil War South, and settled in the Midwest.

He watched the changes in his hometown with interest. The Haverhill he knew in 1830 was not much different from that perceived by young Leverett Saltonstall at the end of the eighteenth century. The population was small and scattered over the sprawling town and numbered almost 2,000 in the 1760s. The 1820 census counted only 1,000 more people. The inland trade and shipbuilding that had sparked growth in the postrevolutionary town had declined in the early decades of the nineteenth century. Like Newburyport and Salem, Haverhill could no longer depend on a mercantile economy.

Boston merchants had already made their move. Prosperity lay in manufacturing, not trade, and manufacturing to them meant textiles. The Merrimack River provided the power, English and Yankee ingenuity provided the machines, the farms of northern New England provided the labor, and Boston provided the capital. Haverhill's domination of the lower Merrimack was challenged in the 1820s by the new town of Lowell, and in the 1840s by a new neighbor on its western flank, Lawrence. Two-hundred-year-old Haverhill watched this transformation, considered its assets, and decided there would be no direct competition with the new textile cities upriver. Industrialization would be encouraged, but, with the exception of Ezekiel Hale's flannel mill on the Little River falls, textiles were not to be the product of choice.

The town's transformation would be the doing of local money, not outside financiers, and would occur according to individual interest, not as nonresident corporations wished. The product would be shoes,

Above: *This sketch depicts Haverhill from the road on the northern bank of the Merrimack, as the village is entered from the east. The Haverhill Bridge is unsurpassed in strength and durability by any structure of its kind in New England. The location of the village is uncommonly beautiful: Haverhill is built on the south side of a gentle acclivity rising from the crescent-shaped river. Courtesy, Trustees of the Haverhill Public Library*

Right: *The east end of Merrimack Street, around 1857, is seen here. The commercial downtown was centered on White's corner, on Water, Main, and Merrimack streets. The upper stories of these brick buildings were often occupied by shoemakers. The street was paved with cobblestones in 1858. Courtesy, Trustees of the Haverhill Public Library*

Above: *A cotton yarn manufactory was begun by Ezekiel Hale at this site on Winter Street next to Little River. He built the peaked-roof brick building seen here in 1835 and began to manufacture scarlet flannel. The factory was sold in 1855 to Stevens and Company, which erected the larger buildings and continued to manufacture cloth well into the twentieth century. Courtesy, Trustees of the Haverhill Public Library*

Left: *Shown here is a trade wagon, of the sort which brought household goods to the farms along the back roads of New England. The peddlers who drove these wagons were a source of communication, carrying news from one community to another. Courtesy, Trustees of the Haverhill Public Library*

Above: *This map of Haverhill, drawn by Henry F. Walling, was published in 1851 by Addison B. Jaques, proprietor of the Haverhill Book Store. It shows the town just prior to its radical transformation into a major industrial city over the next half century. The map includes engravings of these prominent buildings in the village, with the dates they were built (clockwise from left): the new Unitarian church (1848) at the head of the common; the Universalist church (1824) on Summer Street; the first town hall (1846); the new First Baptist Church (1848) on Merrimack Street; the Union Evangelical Church (1839) on Winter Street; the Centre Congregational Church (1834) on Main Street; the Christian church (1824) in Washington Square; and the new Bradford Congregational Church (1848). Courtesy, Trustees of the Haverhill Public Library*

Facing page: *An unidentified Haverhill shoemaker, circa 1900, still used the traditional shoemaking methods which Isaac Merrill had learned in the 1820s. Although nearly all shoe manufacturing was moved into brick factories downtown by the 1870s, there were still many shoemakers who continued to work in their farm shops even into the twentieth century. Courtesy, Trustees of the Haverhill Public Library*

an as yet unmechanized craft. Profits would be made not by manufacturers but by the middlemen who distributed cut stock to independent shoemakers such as Merrill, or in the new shoe shops downtown.

The key to change was the railroad. Merrill's diary recorded the events:

September 5, 1838. *The Directors of the northern railroad met at Col. Tucker's and concluded to commence operations immediately. The building of said road is contracted for. Rufus Slocomb [the express man] has contracted for three miles north of the Merrimack River which carries it to the state line.*

September 15, 1838. *Yesterday, the mud carts and fifty or sixty Irishmen went up to commence working on the railroad soon.*

November, 1838. *Last night one of the Irish children at the railroad died. They kept 12 candles burning all night to light its soul through purgatory. They had grog enough or what is called an Irish wake. The child was carried to Lowell today for burial.*

March 21, 1839. *A Catholic priest from Lowell celebrates or performs a Mass at the Townhouse in Plaistow for the benefit of the Irishmen.*

July 4, 1839. *Young folks of the Parish have fishing dinner in the meadow with powder and wine. Fireworks in the village in evening. Irishmen who belong to railroad had a glorious time getting drunk and feeling quite* pat-riot-ic. *Nobody was killed.*

October 28, 1839. *Today the railroad was finished grading from Bradford to the New Hampshire line.*

January 1, 1840. *The passenger cars commenced running on the railroad from Bradford toward Exeter as far as East Kingston. This road is acceptably reported as being the best in the United States.*

The railroad and the Irish arrived in Haverhill together. Each made an impact that would change the town's appearance and social structure. Of the 5,877 people in Haverhill in 1850, 344 were foreign-born, and 251 alone were from Ireland. Ten years later,

the United States Census reported that out of a total population of 9,995, the number of foreign-born had climbed to 1,274, and 1,000 of that number were Irish.

The railroad tied Haverhill firmly into the Boston and New York markets. The Irish—soon to be followed by the French-Canadians—provided laborers for the brickyards and construction gangs. The railroad also drew another group who came from small towns in Maine, New Hampshire, and Vermont, and were religious and ethnic kin of longtime Haverhill residents. These Yankees filled the shoe shops, retail and wholesale offices, banks, and schools.

The combined influx of Yankees and foreign-born swelled Haverhill's population 302 percent, from 4,336 (1840) to 13,092 (1870). The majority of newcomers found housing where they found work, in downtown Haverhill, the old First Parish by the river.

In 1830 the built-up section of Haverhill extended along the Merrimack River from Kent Street to How Street, and no further upland than Summer and Winter streets. Henry F. Walling's 1851 map of the town shows growth to Mill Street on the east, Dow (now Arlington) Street, White Street, and John Street on the north, to the railroad line on the west. Twenty years later, developers created new neighborhoods as far east as the Town Farm in Riverside. The triangle made by High and Washington streets, west of the railroad, was transformed into Mount Washington, the town's most prestigious address in the 1870s. Here, brick row houses around an open park were reminiscent of Boston's Beacon Hill. The northern edge of the built-up area was now Brickett Street (8th Avenue), the outer border of the Acre. Here the Irish settled and built their first church,

Saint Gregory's, on Harrison Street, and the first signs of urbanized overcrowding became evident. Isaac Merrill recorded the following:

Sunday, December 24, 1854. *In the evening two houses owned by Cornelius Jenness were burnt; situated on the Commons near the village [the present Monument Square area]. Twenty-two rooms in one, occupied by Irish.*

The face of the town had also changed. Public buildings appeared with astonishing regularity in the 1840s and 1850s. These monuments to the citizenry's philanthropy and affluence included the first town hall, built in 1847, and its larger replacement, erected in 1861, and six new churches. The tall tower of the Baptist meetinghouse on Pecker Street was surpassed by the grandeur of the Christopher Wren-like spire of the First Parish church across the river in Bradford. William Brown put a new front on his Main Street hotel, the Eagle House. On Merrimack Street, Caleb Dustin Hunking built a four-story brick block with granite facings, and Charles Carlton and James Duncan, Sr., built a large four-story iron-fronted store. Public monuments were erected to Hannah Duston and veterans of the Civil War.

Even burial grounds were undergoing a change in appearance and perception. Merrill commented:

April 24, 1855. *Went down to the village with J. C. Stuart. We went to Linwood Cemetery and found it a beautiful place. Uncle J. C. Merrill is interred there and has a fine rich monument.*

Merrimack Street was paved and gas lighting in-

Facing page: *The Haverhill (National) Bank issued new paper currency of various denominations in February 1856. All of the bills depict Main Street from White's corner, showing the first town hall, erected in 1846, on the left; the Unitarian church (now the Armenian Apostolic) at the head of the common in the center; and William Brown's newly enlarged Eagle House Hotel on the right. Courtesy, Trustees of the Haverhill Public Library*

Below: *The second town hall was built in 1861 on the site of the first, on Main Street, from a design by John Stevens, a Boston architect. It was entirely gutted by fire in 1888, and rebuilt with different towers. The building continued to serve as city hall until it was torn down during urban renewal in 1973. This photograph was taken circa 1867. Courtesy, Trustees of the Haverhill Public Library*

troduced in the late 1850s. Merrill wrote:

Tuesday, August 24, 1869. *Over 200 stores and tenements have been and are being built at the village this season. The dwellings have the new style of French roofs introduced last year.*

The mansard-roofed buildings that Merrill noted still line the streets today—Cedar, Arlington, and the avenues off Main Street. They were paralleled by identical buildings across the river in Bradford along South Elm, South Pleasant, Middlesex, and South Kimball streets. Overlooking them was the similarly designed Academy Hall in the new location of Bradford Academy.

Change was not only physical but was also institutional. By mid-century Haverhill already had many of the organizations and structures characteristic of an urban environment. A national bank was incorporated in 1814 and a savings bank in 1828. Newspapers had been available since the end of the eighteenth century, the local *Haverhill Gazette* since 1821.

There were few tax-paid town services. Until the 1840s, the choices for education beyond the eighth grade were Atkinson Academy (Merrill's old school), Bradford Academy (1803), or Haverhill Academy (1827), all privately owned. In 1841 the citizens of District One established a high school at the Haverhill Academy building on Winter Street. By 1855, this school served the entire town. The School Street and Winter Street schools, built in 1856, were the first large brick elementary schools in the city.

All other town services were private. Water was provided by the Haverhill Aqueduct Company; the library was the property of the Atheneum Society.

The growth, new buildings, beautification, and civic pride were tied to Haverhill's first great age as a shoemaking center. By 1832 there were some 28 shoe manufacturers throughout the area—middlemen who distributed cut stock to independent shoemakers.

However, the introduction in the 1830s of morocco leather and turned shoes altered Haverhill's shoe fortunes. According to town lore, the first morocco leather came into Haverhill from Danvers and Newburyport. Jess Harding was the first morocco

dresser. Turned shoes were produced by stitching the shoe upper directly to the sole, wrong side out, and then turning the shoe right side out. These products were first made in the Haverhill vicinity by a "tramping jour"—a day worker—who learned the art in Philadelphia and was hired by James Gardner of Bradford to educate others about the secret technique. The introduction of these light, neat, cheap, and fairly durable shoes, in contrast to the heavy and clumsy styles then in use, boosted shoe manufacturing in the town.

By 1850 Haverhill's shoe manufacturers had recovered from the effects of the Panic of 1837. In 1857 there were more than 90 shoe manufacturing establishments and 18 innersole and stiffening plants in operation. Almost all of these factories were located within reach of the Merrimack River and the Boston and Maine Railroad station. In 1860, some 94,000 cases of shoes were produced locally at a value of $3,754,240. One hundred factories, 98 of them making women's slippers, were counted in the 1860 United States Census of Manufactures. Haverhill placed third in the United States, behind Philadelphia and Lynn, in total value of boots and shoes manufactured. Haverhill would retain this dominance for the next 50 years during an era that would completely transform the old town.

When Isaac Merrill reached his destination on Merrimack Street that December morning in 1870, he would have seen the ultimate evidence of Haverhill's transformation—a gaping cellar hole where once the Saltonstall mansion had stood. For almost a century this elegant Georgian structure stood proud amid orchards and sweeping lawns. Now the site was crowded in by multi-storied buildings, and the last male Saltonstall born in Haverhill had moved to Salem.

In 1865 the last wooden building on the south side of Merrimack Street was sold to John C. Tilton and moved to Washington Street below Temple Street. On November 25, 1870, the Saltonstall mansion was moved to the north side of Plug Pond. Two months later, the remaining trees on Merrimack Street were cut down and the entire street turned over to manufacturing interests. A new Haverhill had emerged on what had been the Reverend John Ward's parsonage lands 200 years earlier. The visible past had disappeared.

"YOUR HUMBLE HUSBAND, UNTIL DEATH"

The 28th Regiment of the Massachusetts Volunteer Infantry was one of two regiments raised in the state during the Civil War that totally consisted of Irish immigrants and Irish-Americans. Company H of the 28th was primarily filled by Haverhill men. One of these men was Dennis Ford, who lived with his family near Saint Gregory's Church on Harrison Street.

His early letters home described people and places. Once the fighting started, the letters became tales of survival. Ford and his company fought in a number of major battles, including Second Bull Run, Chancellorsville, Antietam, and Gettysburg.

Hilton Head, South Carolina (undated)

The rebbles are within fifteen miles of us. We don't hear any war news here . . . It is like summer in Ireland only the night air is very bad.

James Island, South Carolina (May 20, 1862)

I can't describe to you the murdres battle that was fought on the 16th. Men fell like grass. I saw four fall with one shot as they were in a line from a cannon. They had a strong fort . . . When we got near them we shouted at them. We shook the Irish flag at them . . . We were butchered like hogs. Our regiment lost 40 or 50 men. All the rest of the Haverhill men are all safe . . . They sware if they get the next chance they will give them ginger.

Newportnuse, Virginia (July 20, 1862)

Send me the childrens likeness. I would feel thankful. They told you the truth. I promised them some money to buy some shoes for John, and Mary a bonnet. I am not forgetting them . . . If I don't go home they will have what I have. Until death. Write soon.

Washington (September 6, 1862)

I have been in four battles since I left Newportnuse . . . The last fight [Chantilly] my clothes was riddled with balls. I was grazed in the wright arm. A ball struck me on the shoe. They fell round me like hail. James Phillips is shot dead. The rest of the boys is safe . . . The war is raging in every direction. The rebbles fight in the woods . . . Let me know how is times in Haverhill. We received no pay for the last two months . . . Our priest can't stand the hardship. We fear he will leave tho he is a smart young man . . . Do you pray for us. Our regiment stood the severest fire that was witnessed. During the war when we got into the woods we ran through what we did not shoot, we beaneted [bayonetted] them. One man begged and got no mercy. A yankey ran him through. Thank God it was not an irish man did it. So I must conclude. I remain your humble husband Dennis Ford until death. I am in hopes I will see Haverhill once more before I die with the help of God.

Maryland Hights Sharpsburgh (October 20, 1862)

We cut the rebbles in the first Maryland fight [South Mountain]. In the second [Antietam] we suffered more than they. I saw of their horses in the last from 14 to 25 killed. The rebbles are brave men. This was the hardest fighting during the war . . . We are whipping them fast. We will soon have them drove back to Richmond. Tell Mrs. McCormick her cosin was killed by the shell that killed [Peter] Donely.

King Street Hospital, Alexandria, Virginia (November 12, 1863)

I was taken prisoner in gatersburgh [Gettysburg], Pennsylvania and was marched to Stanton Virginia. The distance of 200 miles. They starved us with the hunger marching day and night . . . I never fought harder. I did not know where I was when I and six of my company were taken . . . Our Irish brigade was called to the front by the priest. He gave us all absolution. I did not fear. Bullets are hell tho. There was a man shot by my side. I went in twenty yards further than any of the brigade.

Ford was released at some unknown date. He was captured again on August 16, 1864, exchanged on November 27, 1864, and discharged December 19, 1864. He reenlisted with the 14th Battery of the Massachusetts Light Artillery and was sent to Virginia.

Ford was captured a third time on March 23, 1865, paroled on May 20, 1865, and remained in service till the war's end. He returned to Haverhill, where he died in 1868. His widow and children continued to live in the Acre and are buried with Dennis in Saint James Cemetery on Primrose Street.

CHAPTER FOUR

THE QUEEN SLIPPER CITY

When Arthur Harrison Cole was a boy in turn-of-the-century Haverhill, his mother would put him on the trolley that traveled up and down Arlington Street past their home. The lad would be driven to the corner, transferred into the care of the conductor of the Main Street trolley, and let off the electric car when it reached his father's law office in Washington Square.

Years later, in retirement from the Harvard Business School, the renowned economic and business historian recorded his memories in a work entitled *Boyhood in the Golden Age.* The Haverhill he recaptured in his essay has all the shine and attraction of a prized jewel.

The force that pulled Haverhill's diverse neighborhoods together was a trolley system that ran to and from the city's borders. Cole described the influence of the trolley cars:

Automobiles are a disruptive, a sort of dismembering force, if I may use such a figure; each car starts from its individual point of origin and travels its own—or rather—its driver's course. The trolley cars, on the other hand, traced specific well-known and well-established routes for groups of citizens; the patrons on particular routes became socially

This was Washington Square, looking east from Washington Street, as it appeared during Arthur Cole's boyhood in 1906. In 1915 the Haverhill National Bank building replaced the wooden buildings in the center. Courtesy, Trustees of the Haverhill Public Library

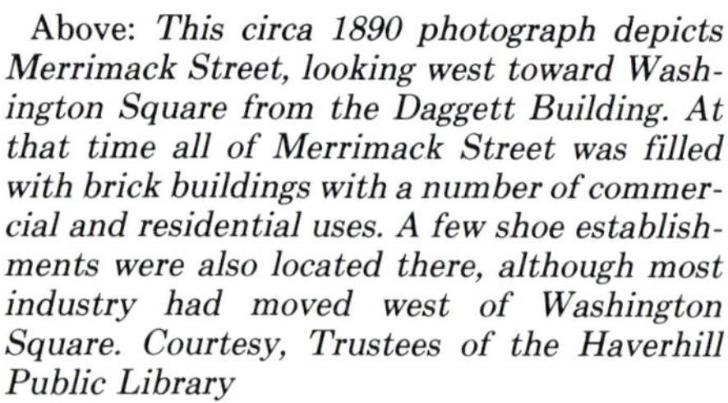

Above: *This circa 1890 photograph depicts Merrimack Street, looking west toward Washington Square from the Daggett Building. At that time all of Merrimack Street was filled with brick buildings with a number of commercial and residential uses. A few shoe establishments were also located there, although most industry had moved west of Washington Square. Courtesy, Trustees of the Haverhill Public Library*

Above right: *One of the most architecturally significant commercial buildings ever erected in Haverhill was the Daggett Building, on Merrimack Street at the corner of Pecker Street. When it was erected in 1888, the building, designed by Haverhill architect C. Willis Damon, was a symbol of the affluence, pride, and commercial importance of downtown Haverhill. One of the last buildings to be torn down under the urban renewal program in 1977, it became a symbol marking the end of the demolition era and the beginning of concern for preservation and restoration. Photo by Thomas Bailey*

Facing page: *The east side of the Highlands neighborhood was rapidly developed in the last 15 years of the nineteenth century with some of the most expensive and architecturally significant houses of Haverhill's Victorian era. Many of these belonged to shoe manufacturers, such as the Queen Anne-style house on the left at 1 Windsor Street. Built in 1887, it belonged to Sylvanus P. Gardner, of the Gardner Block in Railroad Square. The house under construction on the right, at 117 Arlington Street, belonged to another shoe manufacturer, L. Wilder Chase. He was the father of Cora Chase of the Metropolitan Opera Company. Courtesy, Trustees of the Haverhill Public Library*

affiliated with the other 'regulars,' and indeed, with the 'regular' operators of the vehicles.

Bands of growth could be traced between the trolley lines. Three areas of land use are clearly distinguishable on the maps of the period. On the outermost ring lay underdeveloped farmland, open fields, woodlands, and swamps; parishes that had changed little from the way Isaac Merrill knew them.

The innermost band was the old First Parish along the Merrimack River. When Merrill delivered his last case of shoes to Merrimack Street in 1870, that area had just begun its final transformation from a residential to a commercial district. An 1893 bird's-eye map of Haverhill shows the results of that change. A solid mass of red-brick three-, four-, and five-story buildings lined both sides of Merrimack Street. There was not a tree, open spot, park, or public place along the entire length of the street.

Nor had the riverfront been left untouched. Warehouses and small shops filled every space. Even the Baptist church on Pecker Street had disappeared, replaced by the popular Academy of Music. The Baptists moved their congregation to a new Main Street building, not far from Cole's Arlington Street home, built in a style popularized by architect H.H. Richardson, designer of Boston's Trinity Church. Within a few blocks were nine other Protestant churches, including the Calvary Baptist, established for the city's small black community.

The churches had been placed on high ground overlooking and far removed from the busy downtown area. They had followed the population into what constituted Haverhill's third band of land use—a built-up area of residences ranging from mansions to tenements. Most of these houses were built after the Civil War as homes for a population that burgeoned more than 300 percent from 1860 to the end of the century.

The multiplicity of architectural styles can be read as easily as an archaeologist's find. Mansard roofs marked the buildings put up in the immediate postwar period. Single, unadorned Greek Revival structures with gable ends to the street and off-center front doors appeared in the 1870s and 1880s. Exuberant Queen Anne buildings with bow fronts and bay windows, towers and porches, and dormer windows jutting from asymmetrical roofs signaled the growth of the prosperous last decades of the nineteenth century. A century later, their continuing presence is a reminder of how much that era shaped Haverhill's public face.

The boom in home construction eased a similar boom in population growth. Haverhill's population grew from 10,000 in 1860 to 37,000 in 1900. Almost all of that growth was housed within one-and-one-quarter miles of White's Corner, where Water and Merrimack streets met Main Street, and the bridge crossed the river to Bradford. Residence was determined by two things: access to the trolleys and access to work. However, not everyone could afford a daily trolley ride, so development could only spread within walking distance—two miles maximum—of work. Thus, Highlandville grew up on the east side of the Main Street trolley lines while "the Avenues" expanded along the west side, the whole area encompassing all the land between the Kenoza Avenue and Cedar Street lines. Rows of identical multifamily houses were built on new streets within reach of the Washington Street trolleys.

What attracted new population and determined housing patterns and transportation needs was the shoe industry, which permanently defined Haverhill's identity. Its building needs were the most significant shaper of the downtown area's appearance. Its labor needs provided not only the city's primary income but also determined housing and commercial patterns, spawning a myriad of related industrial and business operations.

The 1890 United States Census of Manufactures placed Haverhill third nationwide behind Lynn and Brockton, Massachusetts, in total value of products, wages paid, and capital invested in shoes. An average of 11,000 workers were employed in 236 establishments, and the numbers continued growing for another 20 years.

When young Arthur Cole stepped down from the "electric" in front of his father's law office, he could look across Washington Square into the heart of the shoe industry. If it were not slack time, he could even hear the beat of that heart as thousands of machines cut, stitched, and stamped endless hides of cow and morocco leather. Forty years earlier, Washington Square marked the end of downtown. The first nonresidential structure appeared in 1860 in Washington Square, the Coombs Block. Built at the corner of Emerson Street, it was a graceful Italianate building, intended for shoemaking on a grand scale. Another large block went up in the same area in 1868, and a third, three years later.

A major impetus in the transformation of downtown to a shoe town took place in 1872. J. Porter Gardner decided to build next to the railroad depot, a third of a mile to the west of Washington Square. The building, the largest at that time in the city, was in the new French Empire style, featuring a dormered mansard roof. As more and more shoemakers arrived in town, Gardner wanted his shop to be seen first.

Over the next 10 years, the entire area between

Right and far right: *Josiah M. Littlefield (1826-1917) and C. Willis Damon (1849-1916) were the major architects of Victorian Haverhill. Littlefield designed most of Haverhill's public buildings from 1860-1880, as well as numerous residences and at least one-third of the factories in the Washington Street Shoe District. Damon was the first trained Haverhill architect, graduating from M.I.T. in 1871. His first major job was designing James R. Nichols' Winnekenni Hall in 1873. He is particularly noted for his Queen Anne- and shingle-style residences. Courtesy, Trustees of the Haverhill Public Library*

Below: *The most devastating fire ever in Haverhill leveled nearly 10 acres of shoe factories in the Washington Street section on the night of February 17, 1882. Except for two buildings on the southwest end of the street, all of Washington Street was destroyed, as seen in this photograph looking east toward Washington Square. An estimated 3,000 men and women were temporarily without employment, and 300 shoe firms had to relocate. Courtesy, Trustees of the Haverhill Public Library*

Washington Square and Railroad Square changed from a wooden residential area to a brick-built manufacturing center. Then, in a few hours, it was almost destroyed. During the night of February 17, 1882, fire raged through the shoe district and leveled everything in sight. Only the Gardner Block, and the Currier Block, the furthest building on the riverside of Washington Street, escaped the fire.

Nearly every shoeman affected by the loss had relocated and was back in operation within two days. Within two weeks, the first bricks were laid for new buildings on the old sites. Many of the bricklayers were Italian laborers temporarily imported from New York City and Boston. The bricks were made locally in the brickyards in Haverhill's North Parish and across the border in southern New Hampshire.

In less than a year, the entire district was rebuilt and expanded through Wingate Street, one block north of Washington Street. Each building was an independent undertaking, but most were designed by two local architects, Josiah Littlefield and C. Willis Damon, who followed a common canon of height, composition, and design. What is remarkable about these buildings are their facades. They are museums to the mason's craft. The intricate patterns of brickwork that adorn the upper stories reflect the richness of the Queen Anne style of architecture. Granite, sandstone, contrasting white bricks, and terra-cotta details all added appeal and an enduring beauty.

What permitted such an amazing recovery? How could this comparatively young industry find the economic and personal resources to rebound so quickly? The answer lay in the nature of the shoe industry itself, particularly in Haverhill's version of that industry.

Shoemaking, unlike textile production, required relatively low capitalization. The United Shoe Machinery Corporation held a monopoly on machinery and preferred to lease on a per shoe cost, rather than sell their machines. This removed a major start-up expense for an enterprising shoeman. The process of shoemaking permitted small-scale operations specializing in contract work such as stitching. Because the work was labor intensive, great amounts of floor space were not necessary, nor was permanent space required. The small-scale businesses could be relocated with comparative ease.

The textile cities of Lowell and Lawrence, as well as Manchester, New Hampshire, were large-scale capitalization efforts. Financing came from corporations whose stockholders usually did not have any direct connection with their businesses. In contrast, shoe manufacturing's low capitalization allowed ownership by individuals or two to four partners. These owners lived in the area and made daily appearances at their shops. They were an integral part of the community, serving on boards of trustees for the public library and the YMCA, and holding memberships in the Pentucket Club, the Masonic orders, and the Odd Fellows. Their elegant homes filled the Highlands and lined South Main Street in Bradford.

A city's economic life is measured, however, by more than balance sheets and buildings. Shoes, like other industries, responded to economic barometers. In good times during the 1890s, a stitcher doing piecework could expect to earn $10 a week. In bad times that wage could be cut by a third or more, leaving little for the workers during the June-to-November slump. Business slowed after orders from spring and fall style shows were filled, and workers then had to fend for themselves until factories resumed production.

During the depression years of 1893 and 1894 the Haverhill shoe industry was as affected as any other segment of the economy. A particularly high cost for leather in 1894 added to the pressure on profits. Some shoe manufacturers in Haverhill made a move to save profits by lowering labor costs. The workers resisted, and the result was the Great Haverhill Shoe Strike. From mid-December 1894 to mid-March 1895, during the peak season, more than 3,000 shoeworkers left their machines and filled the streets in protest.

The strike was one of two events that attracted wide public attention. The almost daily reports in the Boston and Haverhill press give us a closer look at the everyday operations of the industry and make it clear that Haverhill was rapidly changing. The industry was moving away from Washington Street. The factories that were affected belonged to the Spauldings and the Chick brothers, a mile west of downtown on River Street. These new utilitarian business blocks operated on a larger production scale than that of the older, smaller shoe shops, and employed the greatest number of workers per factory in the city. Their presence on River Street attracted the newest immigrant groups—Italians,

Workers posed for this photograph in the Chick Shoe Factory at 414 River Street, where many Italian and Jewish immigrants found employment. It was in this factory that the three-month Haverhill Shoe Strike began in December 1894. More than 3,000 workers participated at the height of the strike. Courtesy, Trustees of the Haverhill Public Library

Above: *Seen here is a Haverhill shoe stitching room in the 1890s. Before all shoe operations were combined in one factory, many independent firms had contracts to do the stitching for the shoe manufacturers. This was one area in the shoe industry that was dominated by women, and a majority of the firms were owned by women. Courtesy, Trustees of the Haverhill Public Library*

Facing page: *In 1908 Haverhill became the first community east of the Mississippi River to adopt the commission form of local government. Serving on the first council were, left to right: Alderman John T. Desmond, a civil engineer; Alderman James W. Harris, a bank president; Mayor Edwin H. Moulton, owner of a cold storage company; Alderman Joseph W. Bean, a shoe manufacturer; and Alderman Ubert A. Killam, a bank cashier. Courtesy, Trustees of the Haverhill Public Library*

Armenians, and East European Jews—and greatly increased the population of Ward Five.

In the 1880s and 1890s the majority of shoe-making jobs (cutters, stitchers, and lasters) were held by native-born workers. Many were from northern New England, particularly Maine, a background they often shared with their employers. They carried with them generations of pride and independence, and a tradition of high wages. One estimate suggests that 75 percent of the stitchers at the time of the strike were native-born, most of Anglo-Saxon roots, though some were the children and grandchildren of Irish and Canadian immigrants.

Haverhill's other media event centered on socialism. One leader of the 1894-1895 strike was a young Socialist shoeworker, James Carey, who was known as "Weeping James." This caught the attention of the press and shocked the community, since local socialists did not fit the stereotype. Socialists became a favorite target of the media. Like the new immigrants, they were invariably caricatured as foreign, bearded, wild-eyed bomb-carriers.

However, Haverhill's socialists were in the main, native-born and respectable. Many were involved in the shoe industry. John C. Chase, the first Socialist elected mayor in the United States, ran a cooperative store. Parkman Flanders, mayor in 1903 and again in 1920, was a businessman. Other party members were doctors, ministers, and newspapermen. Their hero was Eugene V. Debs, and their goal was municipal socialism, particularly public ownership of local utilities and higher wages for city laborers.

Chase earned the most publicity, while Carey, a state representative, had the broader field of action. But Flanders, who has often been overlooked, may well have had the longest record of Socialist public service. The long-range impact of the Haverhill Socialist movement confirmed the city's traditional political conservatism and enlisted voters for a solid Republican majority for the next half century.

A more immediate impact brought about major changes in city government. The Socialist Labor Party took temporary control of city government in the wake of public reaction to the 1895 conviction of three aldermen for selling liquor licenses. Caught between scandal and socialism, Haverhill's business community demanded a new city charter. By 1908 a commission form of government was in place.

Haverhill was the first city east of the Mississippi River to adopt the so-called Des Moines, Iowa, model of government, which was a solution to the demand to bring businesslike efficiency and accountability into municipal government. The new system had a powerful mayor and four aldermen, each of whom would be responsible for a major area of government. They would be elected by the city at large and by nonpartisan ballots. This change brought the business community back into government, but it also eliminated the chance for a political machine to develop. This system would remain in place until the post-World War II era.

When Arthur Cole recalled the Haverhill of his youth, he made no mention of strikes, scandals, or Socialists. Such matters were not the proper con-

cern of a well-mannered middle-class boy. What he does recapture for us is everyday life: ice skating on Plug Pond, riding his bicycle to gather mayflowers at John Greenleaf Whittier's birthplace; and playing ball on a vacant lot on Webster Street with the Poindexter boys from Ashland Street. There were summertime picnics by river steamer to Plum Island and Salisbury Beach, trolley excursions to Canobie Lake, the circus' annual visit to the River Street Fairgrounds, and fireworks at the GAR Park on the Fourth of July. Less spectacular were the weekly rounds of singing in the boys' choir at Trinity Episcopal Church, trips to the new Haverhill Public Library for the latest Oliver Optic and Horatio Alger books, and visits to Pong Lee's Chinese Laundry to spend his few spare pennies on litchi nuts.

There were also rounds of chores at home. The coal furnace and kitchen stoves needed regular stoking, and no lad escaped the ordeal of lugging ash barrels to the curb, or rubbing Rising Sun stove polish onto the kitchen stove with vigor. Laundry was done on Monday, ironing on Tuesday, downstairs cleaning on Wednesday, upstairs cleaning on Thursday, and cooking on Saturday. Friday was held in reserve should rain or illness disrupt the routine.

Food preparation was adapted to this schedule, and baked beans, brown bread, and Indian pudding, which all required long slow cooking time, became staples of weekend dining. Meals were planned ac-

Above: *The family of Moses Morris was the first Jewish family to permanently settle in Haverhill. They came from Boston in 1879 and Morris found work at the Guptill Shoe Company as a shoe laster. This photograph, taken around 1904, shows Moses, his wife Maria, and their nine children. As other families came, many arriving between 1902 and 1915, they settled in the River Street area where the first synagogue was established in 1899. Courtesy, Dr. Robert S. Morris*

Right: *The first Greeks came to Haverhill in 1892. By 1930 there were 1,700 persons of Greek descent in the city, with the majority living in the Ward Three area around Winter Street. Nicholas Boukis came to America in 1907 and sent money back to bring his brother Adam over in 1909 and his parents and sisters over in 1913. Pictured is the Boukis family while still in Greece. Sitting with her paternal grandmother Stamatia is Euterpe, the mother of Massachusetts Governor Michael S. Dukakis and the first Haverhill girl of Greek descent to graduate from college. Courtesy, Trustees of the Haverhill Public Library*

Left: *Washington Square, circa 1905, was the major focus of downtown Haverhill, providing a transition between commercial Merrimack Street to the east and industrial Washington Street to the west. Presidents, parades, and celebrations, as well as pedestrians, horses and wagons, and this blind man selling pencils were all a part of the Washington Square scene. Courtesy, Trustees of the Haverhill Public Library*

Below: *This parade, organized by the Ancient Order of the Hibernians for men of Irish descent, was held circa 1900 on Primrose Street. Primrose Street was one of the major roads through the "Acre"—the major Irish neighborhood of the city. On the right is St. James Church, constructed between 1884 and 1896 to serve Haverhill's large Irish Catholic population. Courtesy, Trustees of the Haverhill Public Library*

cording to seasonal availability, which meant that fresh fruits and vegetables were limited. Fish, beef, and mutton were plentiful, but turkey appeared only around Thanksgiving and chicken in late spring. Smoked and salted meats were dietary staples. Cole wrote:

There was also the canning of piccalilli (out of green tomatoes and spices in the early fall); and there was the frying of doughnuts on many a Saturday afternoon. And just before dinner, there might be sweet potatoes baking in the oven, perhaps home-baked Parker House rolls being kept warm in the 'hot' oven at the top of the stove, and even a steak broiling over a bed of red-hot coals. As a youth I rarely ate any food, other than condiments and occasionally ice cream, that was prepared outside the home.

Of 'drink,' in the Cole family, there is little to say. The elders liked their tea and coffee at breakfast and luncheon, and Grandfather went to the trouble of roasting wheat grains in the oven when coffee came to disagree with him. Fruit juices, beyond apple cider for a period in autumn, were almost nonexistent. So also were 'soft drinks,' although Moxie and ginger ale were pushing ahead in popular usage and appeared sometimes in our house. Beers, wines, and, of course, 'harder' liquors were forsworn, largely by reason of Grandfather's connection with the Methodist Church.

Twenty-five years earlier, in 1875, the Massachusetts Bureau of Statistics of Labor surveyed 400 working-class families, many from Haverhill. The one family clearly identified as coming from the city showed eating patterns similar to the Coles' middle-class existence:

No. 79   Shoemaker   American
Earnings of father $496
*   daughter, aged 15 .... 200*
*   son, aged 17 .... 306*
* $1,002*

Condition—Family numbers 7, parents and 5 children from one to seventeen years of age; two go to school besides the eldest girl, who works also four months in the year. Occupy a tenement of 6 rooms, pleasantly situated, with parlor and bed-rooms car-

peted. Have a piano and sewing-machine. Family dresses well and attends church; are in very good circumstances for working people.

Food—Breakfast. Hot biscuits, butter, eggs or meat, sometimes griddle-cakes, cake or pie, bread, tea or coffee.

*   Dinner. Bread, butter, meat, potatoes, vegetables, pudding or pie, cake, pickles and tea.*

*   Supper. Bread, butter, cold meat or cheese, sometimes sauce, cake or pie, tea. Have baked beans two meals a week and fish for dinner once a week.*

Cost of Living $979.47

Rent	$225.00	*Societies*	$16.00
Religion	20.00	*Dry Goods*	26.00
Clothing	96.00	*Boots and*	
Groceries	390.84	* shoes*	22.00
Meat & Fish	72.63	*Sundries, taxes,*	
Milk	28.00	* school-books,*	
Fuel	56.00	* etc.*	27.00

NOTE: Father's wages range from $12 to $16 per week when working; only worked eight months last year. Business has been dull for a year or two. Can not keep family out of earnings. The father had stated that shoemakers earned $18 per week on an average; thought this was not true as far as Haverhill was concerned. Did not earn $10 a week last year, and worked all the time he could, which was about eight months.

Haverhill's Golden Age outlasted Arthur Cole's

In 1874 Winnekenni Hall was built for Dr. James R. Nichols, as a summer residence, on a hill overlooking Kenoza Lake and the farmland on Kenoza Avenue. Nichols used the farmland for chemical agricultural experiments. The "castle" and land were purchased by the city for a park in 1895; with additional land added through the years, the park now contains nearly 250 acres of woodlands for recreation. The "castle" has been leased from the city by the Winnekenni Foundation since 1969, with the intent to restore it and to promote cultural programs on its grounds. Courtesy, Trustees of the Haverhill Public Library

boyhood. Schooling took him from the city to Governor Dummer Academy, Bowdoin College, and Harvard University. He was not able to witness his native city's continued days of glory during the early decades of the twentieth century. From the fire of 1882 until after World War I, Haverhill was a booster's ideal. Growth and prosperity were linked to stability and a clear sense of community. This combination attracted individuals and investment. Population increased 296 percent from 18,172 in 1880 to 53,884 in 1921. Valuations, however, soared 700 percent from $9,201,013 in 1880 to $64,890,531 in 1920, a per capita increase from $506 to $1,204. The tax rate, at the same time, remained consistently around $21 per thousand.

Word spread that Haverhill was a good place in which to live, work, and invest. The message was heard by Gardellas and Carbones in northern Italy, Ornsteens and Starensiers in the old empires of central and eastern Europe, Tavitians from Armenia, and Karambelases from Greece. The news also reached businessmen, including William Bixby, George Lennox, and an enterprising young man from Exeter, New Hampshire, Louis Hamel.

The population became more and more heterogeneous, a cosmopolitan mix drawn from four continents. Though never a true immigrant city, Haverhill's population increasingly reflected more and more immigrant connections. In 1900 the population of 37,175 was almost evenly divided between children born of native parents (18,654) and those who were either foreign-born or had parents who were foreign-born (18,151). Fifteen years later, the latter group outnumbered the former, 28,648 to 20,363.

The greatest number of immigrants to Haverhill, according to every census since 1900, claimed Canada as a homeland. This includes not only the expected high number of French-Canadians from Quebec and Nova Scotia but also English-speaking natives of Prince Edward Island and the other Maritime Provinces. Because this latter group did not gravitate to specific churches or social groups, as the French-Canadians, Irish, Italians, and Greeks did, and because their names did not readily identify their place of origin, they have remained a hidden, assimilated part of the population.

The shoe shops absorbed most of the population increase. Almost 12,000 people were employed in the industry in 1917. But family biographies show that a surprising number of newcomers went into business for themselves. The majority went into the shoe industry, which required little capital. Other newcomers sought independence by opening their own fruit and vegetable stores, meat markets, and restaurants. The first half of the twentieth century became the era of the neighborhood store.

Haverhill attracted people of vitality and risk. City government responded to this growth with energy and adventurousness. From 1880 to 1920 the city underwent its greatest public changeover, which would not be matched in scope and vision until the last quarter of the twentieth century.

The city's service expenditures increased more than 300 percent, from $654,125 in 1891 to $2,016,374 in 1921. The greatest part of that expense was earmarked for schools and health. A new high school was built in 1908 and new red-brick schools ap-

peared in every part of the city. Their names—Wood, Moody, Fox, Bartlett, Peabody, Knipe, Smiley, and Crowell—were memorials to city leaders of the era. Additional public schools would not be built for the next 40 years. Health care was handled by the new Hale Hospital on Buttonwoods Avenue, which replaced the original Kenoza Avenue building. In addition, by 1920 Haverhill boasted the Gale Hospital for the sick and injured, a Contagious Hospital, a Tuberculosis Hospital, a City Dispensary, and a full-scale school health program regularly serviced by doctors, dentists, and nurses.

The turn of the century was also the age of the City Beautiful and the Garden City movements, which Haverhill enthusiastically joined. With great foresight for the preservation of Haverhill's spectacular natural beauty, the city authorized the establishment of a park department in 1890. The heart of the park system was the Kenoza Lake-Winnekenni Castle-Plug Pond green space. In 1909, a citywide playground network was created and placed under the park department's aegis. Haverhill became a model of progress, but not at the expense of its community.

Amid the growth and change, one significant event still stirs debate today—the annexation of Bradford. The issue had been a topic of lively interest and intermittent electioneering for 30 years, but the outcome was inevitable. Annexation was a very popular movement in post-Civil War America when size was equated with power. By the end of the nineteenth century, Bradford had become a residential community for Haverhill's businessmen and professionals. Haverhill, in turn, provided employment, services, and entertainment for Bradford's population.

Bradford's history is as long established as Haverhill's, but its development followed a different route. It had no open territory to expand into, no hinterland to draw upon. Thus, trade went to Haverhill in the eighteenth and nineteenth centuries, while Bradford remained small and pastoral, with only a few small mills and some domestic manufacture. The town developed two centers, one at the bridge opposite downtown Haverhill, the other further east by the Chain Ferry. By 1851 the two sections had grown so much apart that the East Parish of Bradford requested, and was granted, separation by the Massachusetts General Court as a new town, Groveland. After that the remaining portion of Bradford was drawn even closer to its neighbor across the river. The railroad, the bridge, and the trolley reinforced their economic and social ties.

There was resistance to annexation, spawned by love of independence and pride of place. But what probably tipped the scale was an action that was a direct result of the great fire of 1882. One merchant displaced by the disaster was an English-born contract shoe shop owner, William A. Knipe. He chose to relocate from Washington Street to a spot in rural Ward Hill, in the southern end of Bradford. There, next to a railroad line, he built not only a factory but a village. Between Boston Road and the railroad a pattern of new streets was laid out, filled with single and multifamily houses, a boarding house, and a store. The new factory and the houses were built of wood, and Knipe held title to them all. Ward Hill became as close to a company town as any area in Haverhill's experience.

The rapid growth of the Ward Hill section coincided with a growing demand in the region for public services. Ward Hill wanted water lines, sidewalks, and paved streets, but the two-mile distance from Knipe's new development meant an extraordinary outlay of funds that budget-conscious Bradford selectmen could neither favor nor afford. The Knipes then turned to Haverhill. In 1896 a petition requesting the General Court to permit a vote on annex-

ation was headed by William Knipe and his sons. The petition and subsequent election were successful, and on January 1, 1897, Bradford bade farewell to its independence. However, the diehards had the last word. A black-bordered obituary appeared in the *Haverhill Evening Gazette*:

Mother Bradford died suddenly of an overdose of damphoolishness at midnight on November 3, aged 225 years. She left a will bequesting all her vast domains to her big sister across the river. Being of unsound mind the will may be contested. The burial will take place on January 1. Kind friends will please send forget-me-nots.

Grand old Bradford, thou hast left us,
   And our Loss we deeply feel
But 'tis fools which hast bereft us
   How we'll laugh to hear them squeal.

            A Mourner.

Right: *Neighborhoods near the downtown were served by numerous stores of all types and sizes. A major one on the edge of the Acre was the White Street Market, located at 114-118 Winter Street in the Killam Block. Owned by G. Herbert Thurston, this market included four departments, a bakery, and a delivery service. It operated between 1887 and 1913. Courtesy, Trustees of the Haverhill Public Library*

Facing page: *Ayers Village, named primarily for John Ayer who moved this hat-making business there in 1801, developed during the nineteenth century as another "village within the town." At its peak, the village had over 50 residences, 4 hat factories, 2 shoe shops, 2 stores, a post office, a fire house, a church, a school, a blacksmith shop, and a community hall. When the hat industry became more mechanized in the 1860s and 1870s, the manufacturers moved their concerns to Washington and River streets. Courtesy, Trustees of the Haverhill Public Library*

THE STRANGE CAREER OF GEORGE LAWRENCE DAY

In the 25th anniversary report of the Harvard College class of 1893, there appears the notation "Lost" beside the name of George Lawrence Day. Day's strange story begins with an incident involving the statue of John Harvard in Harvard Yard. The statue was vandalized with a coat of crimson paint by two students following Harvard's football victory over Yale. Day, one of two suspects, left his dormitory, hurried home to Haverhill, and then disappeared. He would periodically reappear dressed in military uniform and hardly recognizable. Then he would vanish again for long periods of time during which even his own family lost all track of him.

The Day family lived at No. 42 (now No. 146) Summer Street in the Highlands section of the city. The double brick house was set off by spacious terraced lawns. The father, George Whitfield Day, was a local shoe manufacturer.

The Day Homestead on Summer Street was shared by the Day brothers, George and Luther. This 1878 photograph shows the brick Greek Revival-style house. Courtesy, Trustees of the Haverhill Public Library

"Chick" Day, as George Lawrence was known, attended the School Street School and Haverhill High School. He entered Harvard College in 1889 after showing great prowess as a pitcher on the Phillips Exeter Academy baseball team. Then came the unproved college prank.

Accompanied by another student, Day shipped on a cattle boat for Europe. Stranded in London without funds, the boys received money from Day's father for their passage home. On his return, Day apparently enlisted as a seaman under his own name in the United States Navy. He later joined the United States Marine Corps under the name John Mapes Adams. It was common knowledge among his company that he had enlisted under an assumed name.

In China during the Boxer Rebellion, Day was one of 30 marines who volunteered to scale the walls of Tientsin. Unable to succeed in their objective, they withdrew under heavy fire. The captain who commanded the assault was pinned down and wounded on the field of battle and was rescued by Day. The U.S. Navy Department awarded the Medal of Honor to Day for "distinguished conduct in the presence of the enemy in battle near Tientsin, China, July 3, 1900."

Day was discharged in 1902. The story goes that William H. Moody of Haverhill, Secretary of the Navy in President Theodore Roosevelt's cabinet, learned that the "Sergeant Adams" who received the Medal of Honor was a local boy. Moody tried to help Day get a commission, which apparently was not to Day's liking. Day reenlisted in the Marine Corps in 1902 under the name of Adams, but named his real mother as his next-of-kin.

Day was discharged in 1909. Six years later he enlisted in the Army at Fort Howard, Maine, and was discharged in 1917 to accept a commission as a second lieutenant. He met Stella Isabel Joyce, a nurse from Peekskill, New York, and married her in Newport, Rhode Island. Shortly thereafter Day was shipped overseas to serve with the Allied Expeditionary Forces.

He returned to the United States in October 1919, suffering from a nervous condition complicated by an attack of influenza. When he recovered, he reenlisted as a first sergeant at Fort Slocum, New York, and was assigned to Fort Wadsworth, New York, where he died of heart failure in his wife's arms in 1920. Day was buried in the Brooklyn National Cemetery under the name of John Mapes Adams. It was then discovered that Adams was George Lawrence Day, a native of Haverhill and holder of the Medal of Honor— "an extraordinary, intrepid soldier, whose life read like a storybook."

After the publication of John Greenleaf Whittier's masterpiece Snowbound in 1866, his home, the old Haverhill Homestead, became a pilgrimage destination for numerous Americans. This painting by a local artist and friend of Whittier, Obed Fowler, was made from an 1849 sketch by the artist. It shows the old house, begun in the 1680s and later added to, as well as the barn and the old blacksmith shop where Whittier made slippers to earn the tuition money to attend Haverhill Academy. The homestead has been open to the public since 1893. Courtesy, Trustees of the Haverhill Public Library

Above: *Fifteen years after Mrs. Green's original sketch of Haverhill, she drew an updated view to be included in Mirick's "History of Haverhill," published in 1832. It showed a number of changes, including the new Academy Building on Winter Street; the new Summer Street, cut parallel to Water but farther up the hill in the Highlands; and the Jarvis Block on Stage Street. More brick blocks appeared on both Water and Merrimack streets, and the only shipyard left in the village was Barnard Goodridge's, at the base of How Street. Courtesy, Trustees of the Haverhill Public Library*

Left: *The Haverhill City Hospital opened its doors on December 29, 1887, in the renovated Franklin Brickett House—Midlake Farm—located, as seen here, between Round Pond (on the left) and Kenoza Lake (on the right). Its name was changed to Hale Hospital in 1898, in honor of E.J.M. Hale, who proposed the building of a hospital and left money and land for that purpose. In 1901, concern about hospital contamination reaching the city's water supply, Kenoza Lake, caused a new facility to be built on Buttonwoods Avenue. It remained open until 1984. This 1873 painting was the work of Harry E. Remick, a draftsman in the architectural office of J.M. Littlefield. Courtesy, Trustees of the Haverhill Public Library*

Facing page, top: *Mitchell's Falls blocked navigation beyond Haverhill, and although numerous plans for bypassing the rocks were proposed, nothing worked. This area had been an Indian crossing place and fishing location for centuries. During the Indian trouble of the late seventeenth and early eighteenth centuries, militiamen were stationed on the hills overlooking these falls to watch for Indians. Painting by Obed Fowler. Courtesy, Howard W. Curtis*

Left: *Washington Square was captured at night in this Justine Hill photograph.*

Facing page: *Bradford Common, at the junction of the two main roads through Bradford—leading to Salem and to Boston—was the site of the third meetinghouse for the Bradford Church, from 1751 to 1834. The church and common are the visual center of the Bradford Common Historic District, comprising some 90 structures in every architectural style. Established in 1975, the district was placed in the National Register of Historic Places in America in 1977. This church building has served the parish of the First Church since 1848. In the 1920s its design was copied by Henry Ford, and used for his Martha and Mary Chapels. Photo by David J. Joyall. Courtesy, Trustees of the Haverhill Public Library*

Below: *Boating is a popular pastime on the many lakes and rivers in and around Haverhill.*

X-RAY
DR. D.N. SHORT
DENTIST
W. F. THAYER.
ROSENGARD'S
THE BULL MORRIS PLAN CO.

CHAPTER FIVE

THE ROLLER COASTER YEARS

P rivate First Class Serafino R. Tedesco, in France with the American Expeditionary Force, received a letter from home in March 1919 from his younger brother, Anthony, a student at Harvard.

This is Saturday afternoon and I am going to meet a friend of mine. He is an Italian named Paul Gardella from Haverhill whose father is a shoe manufacturer . . . they make McKay shoes 100% and evidently make a good deal of money out of it. Their factory is a small one as its capacity is but 150-200 pairs a day. I have been up there and spent a weekend at their home which is very beautiful. They have two automobiles and two maids. Of course this only goes to show how much you can do by being in business for yourself . . . We must see what we can do about starting up a very small shoe factory. There is absolutely no reason why we cannot do it.

How concisely the letter captures the lure of the shoe industry. The business' easy road to success had drawn new blood and new money into Haverhill for decades. The younger Tedesco's dreams of glory were no different from those of the small-town Mainers who flocked to Haverhill

Throughout Haverhill's history there have been numerous floods, or "freshets," usually in early spring. The most devastating flood took place in March 1936, when the Merrimack River peaked at 30 feet above sea level. The people in this photo were evacuating items from the second floor of the Franklin Block on Merrimack Street by Washington Square. Courtesy, Trustees of the Haverhill Public Library

Left: *Sporting its distinctive box shape, hip roof, and front porch, the structure known as the "Haverhill House" was found in nearly every Haverhill neighborhood. This particular house was one of several built on Lexington Avenue as part of a speculative development project after the turn of the century. Courtesy, Trustees of the Haverhill Public Library*

Facing page: *This temporary "fresh air hospital" near Lake Kenoza was used for influenza patients at the end of World War I. A group of nurses is pictured here in front of the hospital. Courtesy, Trustees of the Haverhill Public Library*

in the nineteenth century. Turn-of-the-century growth had continued unabated, and by the second decade of the twentieth century the city's expansion had been dubbed the Million Dollar Construction Program. From 1911 through 1917, the cost of construction averaged a million dollars a year. Some ten million dollars had been spent on shoe factories alone since 1903.

New block-long factories sprang up where the railroad tracks crossed Winter Street. On Essex Street, near the place where Patrick Driscoll's boardinghouse and tavern had welcomed new Irish immigrants, the world's largest concrete shoe factories were built. Domestic construction was dominated by the introduction of the single-family Haverhill House.

The shoe business and the growing number of related industries continued to dominate Haverhill's economy. Of 16,000 wage earners in the city in 1919, 75 percent were dependent on the shoe industry for their livelihood. Government contracts during World War I had given an added boost to production and increased employment to new highs.

This optimism had surfaced in the immediate aftermath of World War I. Haverhill had more than 4,000 men and women in uniform in 1917-18, half of them serving overseas. More than 100 were killed, 200 wounded. Over 100 medals were awarded. On the home front, nearly 1.3 million dollars was raised in Liberty Loan drives, Red Cross campaigns, and other united war effort drives. Not since the fire of 1882 had so much been asked of Haverhill's residents in such a short time.

The worldwide influenza epidemic at the war's end had also taken a toll. The number of cases strained medical resources and required the use of Camp Kenoza, a temporary "fresh air hospital," at the lake of that name. Having survived war and pestilence, anything seemed possible.

By the early 1920s, epidemics were a part of the past. So, it appeared, were the prospects for the shoe industry. Serafino Tedesco returned to civilian life, married the girl next door, and, by 1923, had made it to Haverhill, but not as an independent businessman. Instead, he became the superintendent for the Moss Seaman Company on Essex Street, a firm owned by nonresidents of the city. Paul Gardella's father, Joseph, whose success had encouraged Serafino's younger brother in 1919, no longer had his own business and had also become an agent for a firm whose owner lived in Boston. What was once a "sure thing" had begun to stir up some disturbing questions about the performance of the shoe industry and, in particular, how a city based on a one-industry economy survives change.

Enough questions had been raised by 1928 to make the United States Department of Labor send a team of economists and labor statisticians to the city to find out what was going on. In its report on the "Conditions in the Shoe Industry in Haverhill, Mass., 1928," the committee concluded that the shoemaking process and the consumer's demands had been revolutionized, but management and labor were locked in an out-of-date mind set.

Haverhill's history from the 1920s to the 1960s was deeply affected by these conflicts within the shoe industry. From the early years, Haverhill shoe manufacturers concentrated on the production of women's turned shoes. This led, in turn, to the establishment of a number of secondary manufacturers, who produced bows, buckles, buttons, straps, beads, and other accessories. Sales depended on a capricious buying public, whose whims shoe designers tried to anticipate twice a year.

With the 1907 introduction of a wood heel covered in celluloid in many styles, colors, and heights, the McKay novelty shoe production in Haverhill increased rapidly. The city became the world center of wood-heel production, but this shift placed a premium on the low cost of manufacture. The four main elements of cost were materials, labor, transportation, and the competition prompted by Haverhill's success. Foreign firms, such as T&A Bata of Czechoslovakia, began using American technology to turn out a cheaper shoe with cheaper labor. This was a specific threat to Haverhill, whose labor costs were the proximate cause of the city's roller coaster shoe production.

The threat of foreign competition and increased domestic competition was compounded by the revolution in women's fashions in the 1920s. The dramatic change from the demure, prewar Gibson girl to the jazz-age flapper meant not only new wardrobes but new shoes for every occasion and every season.

In 1923 Haverhill was the major center of McKay novelty women's footwear, boasting two-thirds of American production. The city was the wood-heel center of the world. The largest plant was the Slipper City Wood Heel Company, which turned out 24,000 pairs of heels per day. The 1920s saw Haverhill shift from the Queen Slipper City of America to the Queen Shoe City. In 1925 Edwin Newdick, chairman of the Haverhill Shoe Board and chief arbiter of shoe wages, pointed out:

It is easy to see why Haverhill is somewhat of an industrial barometer. It is a one industry town—

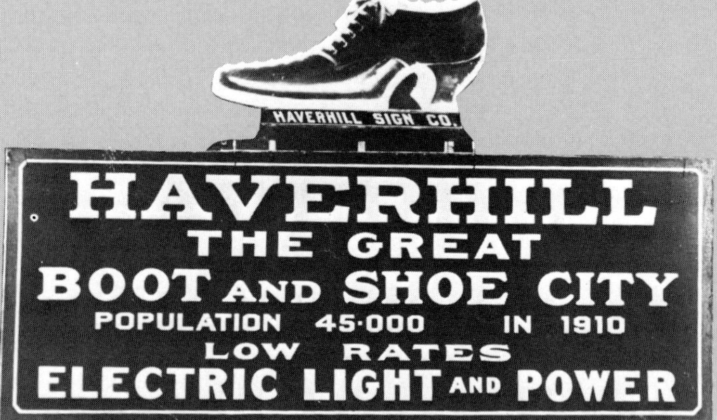

HAVERHILL SIGN CO.
HAVERHILL
THE GREAT
BOOT AND SHOE CITY
POPULATION 45·000 IN 1910
LOW RATES
ELECTRIC LIGHT AND POWER

shoes. In Haverhill one catches early glimpses of change occuring in one of New England's greatest industries because there is nothing in the city, industrially speaking, to dilute or befog the evidence.

No wonder, then, that by 1928, the city was in economic crisis. There were 122 shoe firms in business on January 1, 1920. Nine years later, 102 businesses were in production. but in the intervening years, 219 firms either went out of business or moved, usually to southern New Hampshire, where no labor unions dared enter. The distance from Haverhill to centers of population raised transportation costs. In addition, women's novelty shoes required more stitching, raising the piece-rate cost of each pair. Pressure of competition and unpredictability of sales put a high premium on keeping manufacturing costs as low as possible especially the cost of labor, which was the only factor that Haverhill shoe manfacturers could reasonably control.

Manipulation of wages meant negotiating with the Shoe Workers Protective Union (SWPU), a loose amalgam of local craft unions with no national structure. Organized by firms, process, and operation, each local was directed by agents or secretary/treasurers, who approved the wage lists in tandem with the shoe manufacturers and an overseeing arbitration system.

However, it was not hours that dictated wages but the number of pieces each worker could produce per day. Contracts between each firm and each union dealt with costs in hundredths of cents per unit per total hours worked. Rate books were fat and unwieldy and required constant editing and updating. The result was a kind of short-term mentality on the part of both labor and management, with constant labor unrest as the 1920s shoe market grew more unpredictable.

The Haverhill Shoe Manufacturers' Association (HSMA) was formed to organize the process by which prices were established for labor costs. The real crisis between the HSMA and the SWPU was related to signing a contract before or after the price list of shoes had been agreed upon. This was critical, for the shoes in the spring and fall shows would be priced on a projected cost-per-unit basis by orders received. The SWPU asserted its demands under the constant threat of a strike. Shoemen responded

Above: *The hustle and bustle of Merrimack Street is depicted in this photograph, circa 1940. Courtesy, Trustees of the Haverhill Public Library*

Facing page, top: *During the 1910s and into the 1920s, Haverhill reached new heights in population, in industrial growth, in wealth, and in the number of shoes produced. This promotional sign, advertising Haverhill as a good community in which to locate, stood on Boston Road in the Ward Hill section. Courtesy, Trustees of the Haverhill Public Library*

Facing page, bottom: *The manufacturing of shoes as a distinct industry has been a part of the Haverhill economy for nearly 200 years. Looking at some examples in the large collection at the Haverhill Historical Society in 1957 were Saul Shain of the Nova Shoe Company and Betty Look, Historical Society Curator. Courtesy, Trustees of the Haverhill Public Library*

Above: *The members of the 1936 Haverhill High School championship football team look enthusiastic about the season's successes. Courtesy, Trustees of the Haverhill Public Library*

Facing page: *One of the major WPA projects in Haverhill was the construction of the cement football stadium in Riverside. This photograph, taken December 19, 1936, shows the back of the stands and the new wall built with bricks from the Lennox and Briggs factory on Locke Street, which burned in 1935. Courtesy, Trustees of the Haverhill Public Library*

by simply packing up and leaving the city.

Haverhill's temporary solution to the labor-management conflict was to shift the burden of decision-making to third parties—either arbitration councils of citizens or, in a bold move, to a permanent arbiter, a paid position usually offered to a professional negotiator or labor economist. This latter move was an industry innovation that gained nationwide attention as the Haverhill Experiment. Liberals hailed it as a giant step forward in labor relations.

Working conditions were deteriorating. Curtis P. Sanborn, head of the local of one shoe company, vividly outlined conditions at his factory. The departments at the shop were overcrowded. Machines blocked entrances and aisles. Toilets and other cleaning facilities were extremely unsanitary; sewage often backed up in pipes and overflowed onto the floor.

Sanborn's comments were heard in the aftermath of a major strike in 1933, when 100 percent of the city's shoeworkers were out for three weeks. Such were the vagaries of the industry that within days of his complaints, the *Haverhill Evening Gazette* told of buyers flocking to the city for summer shoes, of six plants operating third shifts, and of overtime at a four-year high.

Success had been a way of life for so many years in Haverhill that residents found it difficult to accept decline. On April 11, 1930, the *Haverhill Evening Gazette* printed a letter from an optimistic citizen who signed himself "Progress."

Haverhill is in just the right position to make the shoes which will be sold in number hereafter among the women as the factories know how to make these shoes, how to put the style into them, how to make them look like the higher-priced shoes, with the same fine lines, how to make the light edges and shapely heels, and put in the clever workmanship. From every viewpoint, the whole looks good in all features and the only fly in the ointment is the great number of other factories all over the country and more in the future than ever before.

Over the next decades, the voice of "Progress" would be joined by others certain that Haverhill could still dominate in the industry so long linked to its name.

It would be too easy to tell Haverhill's history during the years between the wars as if all that mattered was the shoe industry. Those who lived through the years remember people, events, and places and recall a Haverhill where everyday life did matter.

Saturday, June 14, 1924, was fair with moderate winds, according to the *Haverhill Evening Gazette*. The rain that had postponed the baseball game between Haverhill and Lawrence high schools had stopped. The Council of Jewish Women were planning a picnic at Canobie Lake the next day. The Elks Club was holding Flag Day exercises at eight. Those looking for livelier entertainment could find dancing at Conley's Grove, the Hampton Beach Casino, and Canobie Lake Park. The 44 young men and women who were to graduate from Saint James High School the following afternoon were probably at home preparing for the great event.

At the Strand Theatre, a poster for the silent photodrama "By Divine Right" promised "big thrills,

greater emotions, pathos, power, and divinity." Or for 10 cents, 15 cents, or 20 cents (plus tax), the Colonial Theater presented Norma Talmadge in "The Song of Love."

Traditional Saturday night supper featured fresh, corned, or smoked shoulder at 12 ½ cents a pound from Nelson Brothers' Market on Water Street. Chicken was still a luxury at 38 cents a pound. If mother did not want to cook, Butler's on Fleet Street sold baked beans at 25 cents a quart and freshly baked brown bread in four sizes.

Stay-at-homes could listen to the still-new radio, though choices of broadcasts were few and all stations carried a similar format. WBZ in Boston offered dinner-dance music by Ted Reisman and his orchestra, broadcast direct from the Palm Room of the Hotel Lenox. With some manipulation, the listener might pull in KDKA from East Pittsburgh, Pennsylvania.

The Reverend Clark Brownell, D.D., pastor of the First Baptist Church, prepared his sermon, "Some Ancient Landmarks," while Miss Rowell and Miss Pond rehearsed their duet of "Whispering Hope," which they would sing at the 10:30 a.m. service at the Centre Congregational Church the next day.

Harry Pethybridge and his son William embarked on a summer tour of the Midwest. Edna Douglas finished her freshman year at Bates College. A birthday party, complete with a Jack Horner

pie as centerpiece, was given for four-year-old Thomas Melvin Cooke II.

Haverhill survived the 1930s Depression. The many small shops proved more resilient than Lawrence and Lowell's great corporations. Banks and businesses failed, wages and hours were cut. Mayor George Dalrymple (1933-1939), a shoeman himself, practiced strict fiscal conservatism while coping with increasing pleas for public relief.

In 1936 Haverhill had 7,500 wage earners, 5,600 of whom were employed in the shoe industry. This was 31 percent fewer than the high employment numbers of the early 1920s. The average annual wage declined from $1,187 in 1925 to $909 in 1936, a 23-percent drop. The population remained steady, numbering from 48,000-50,000 throughout the decade. The lack of flight from the city suggests an underlying strength to the economy. In 1935, 15.4 percent of the population (7,648) was receiving some form of relief, a rate that compares favorably with regional and national figures.

In 1932 Haverhill broke with its long-standing Republican tradition and, by the slimmest of majorities (8,788 to 8,749), voted for Roosevelt's New Deal. Though the Democratic party was still 20 years away from controlling city government, the benefits of the New Deal were welcomed by the incumbent administrations. More than 2.5 million dollars in relief aid, supporting 488 projects, was re-

Facing page, left and right: Two Haverhill men who gave their lives in combat—one the son of the mayor, the other the son of a Haverhill architect—were commemorated in the book Haverhill In World War II. *The book includes similar sketches of all who died in the war, as well as a listing of those who served and a full record of the activities of the community in support of the war effort.*

Below: Company A is pictured at the Haverhill Armory on Kenoza Avenue in the fall of 1940. On December 23, 1940, the company was called to active service as part of the 182nd Massachusetts Infantry, which served throughout the duration of World War II until deactivated on December 2, 1945. Some 6,500 Haverhill men and women saw active duty in all branches of the service. Courtesy, Trustees of the Haverhill Public Library

ceived by 1937. The new stadium on Lincoln Avenue and the new post office in Washington Square were two significant results. An additional million dollars paid for the construction of a seawall along the Merrimack River in the downtown area. Seasonal flooding had been tolerated since the town was founded, but damage from the great flood of 1936 made a barrier essential. Ninety-nine percent of the laborers on the seawall project were local residents, and their wages were put into local coffers via grocery stores, gas stations, and taxes.

One other factor may help to explain Haverhill's ability to survive the depression years. The 1940 census revealed that 37.3 percent of all houses in Haverhill were owner-occupied, reflecting a stable society and a preponderance of single-family homes. This rate was almost twice that of Boston (20.9 percent) and above the state average of 34.9 percent. The same census revealed that the average rent was $25 a month, an affordable payment for a wage earner at then-current incomes.

The roller coaster that Haverhill rode in the 1930s was tame in comparison to the emotional upheavals of the 1940s. The impact of World War II reached into all levels of life. From Pearl Harbor to Hiroshima, Haverhill's residents responded in overwhelming numbers to the national demand for manpower and financial aid. Sixty-five hundred men and women donned uniforms, 65 percent of them in the army.

A list of those who served mirrors Haverhill's ethnic mix. It includes 42 Smiths, 34 Comeaus, and 33 Sullivans, reflecting the city's three longest residing groups—English, French-Canadian, and Irish. However, the ranks of the dead best reflect the growing diversity of the city's population. One hundred and fifty-four Haverhill men made the ultimate sacrifice.

Seaman 1/c Matthew J. Augusta was killed on November 13, 1942, when his ship, the USS *Monssen,* engaged the Japanese off Savo Island near Guadalcanal in the Solomon Islands.

Sergeant John N. Boyajian was mortally wounded during the Anzio campaign in Italy as a member of Company A, 179th Infantry Regiment, 45th Infantry Division.

Patrick P. Linnehan enlisted in the Navy in 1943. Six months later he was officially presumed dead after his ship was attacked at anchor in Italy.

Aerial gunner Harold H. Santarelli died in 1944 when his B-24 crashed near Port Moresby, New Guinea.

First Lieutenant Clinton P. Goodwin, Jr., served with the 777th Tank Battalion. He died on April 22,

1945, in Eilenburg, Germany, when his tank received a direct hit.

Rifleman Orazio Emilio was one of four brothers to serve in the Army. He was killed during house-to-house fighting in southern France on August 16, 1944.

Sergeant Melvin Peck was killed on January 13, 1944, during the advance on Rome. Three months later, his brother, Private Charles Peck, met a similar fate at Anzio. Private Peter Loucopoulos died in a truck accident in Colorado on June 4, 1943. In the same month, his younger brother Charles graduated from Haverhill Trade School and was killed fifteen months later in Italy.

Perhaps one of the most poignant deaths was that of Captain William D. Glynn, United States Marine Corps, on July 26, 1944, while landing with his men on the beach at Guam. A graduate of Haverhill High School in 1938 and the United States Naval Academy in 1942, he attracted publicity not only because of his good looks but because his father, Albert, was city mayor from 1939-1949. Mayor Glynn's personal grief had to be privately expressed because of the enormous public demands on the citizenry. War contracts, civil defense, fund-raising, and social service needs engaged the energies of a great part of the home population.

The first war contract in the city, for 300,000 emergency medical kits, was awarded on October 5, 1940 to J&A Shoe Company. Many contracts followed for ammunition bags, puttees, invasion jackets, cartridge belts, seabags, and jungle packs. At peak production, there were about 2,500 stitchers at work, 90 to 95 percent of whom were women. In all, 130 establishments used women for as much as 50 percent of the jobs.

Machine shops were next to win contracts. The A.H. DuGrenier Company, a manufacturer of vending machines, was awarded an Army "E" for excellence in the production of firing pins for the Browning automatic rifle.

August 1943 saw a major event in Haverhill's war effort and future economic history. Western Electric Company decided to open shops in Haverhill for the production of coils and transformers to be used in radar, radio, and telephone systems. Empty buildings were stocked and by December 1943, 500 employees were at work. Six months later that number had swelled to 1,900 workers, including both men and women from ages 16 to 60. By war's end, more than 2,000 machinists, engineers, winders, and bench hands worked for Western Electric. The future had arrived in Haverhill.

The effects of four years of war included food shortages, air-raid drills, and blackouts. War bond drives raised over $26 million and drew celebrities to the city, such as film star Dorothy Lamour. School children bought liberty stamps and collected tin cans and aluminum foil. In the fall of 1944, city schools engaged in a massive collection of milkweed pods used to fill life jackets.

Calvary Baptist Church provided Haverhill's first chaplain to the military, the Reverend Robert J. Smith. Scoutmaster Robert D. Malcolm of the First Universalist Parish led the region in blood donations with 17 pints, one for each of his scouts in the service. The combined parishes of Saint Rita's ("the Italian church") and Saint George's ("the Lithuanian church"), both located in Ward Five, saw 1,300 people join the service, 21 of whom died in action.

In Ayers Village, Sarah Stover reacted to the news of Pearl Harbor by setting up the Navy Knitters. By war's end, over 1,000 volunteers had created almost 20,000 knitted socks, scarves, mittens, sweaters, and watch caps and distributed them to sailors, marines, coastguardsmen, and merchant seamen.

The war ended on August 15, 1945, and two days later the first war contracts were cancelled. Companies laid off 5 to 100 percent of their workforce. The Haverhill Chamber of Commerce anticipated the future with great optimism. The city's industry had reached the diversification that had been sought for years.

Haverhill needed to erect new factories specially designed for heavier industry, as well as modernize existing space and rehabilitate commercial fronts and interiors. Diversification also required a city-controlled airport, additional parking facilities, better roads, and housing for war veterans. Chamber officials were confident that Haverhill's industry would help meet the needs of the post-war world, and that the skill of its workers and spirit of its citizens would keep the city in the forefront. Only time would tell if Haverhill had learned the lesson of its past.

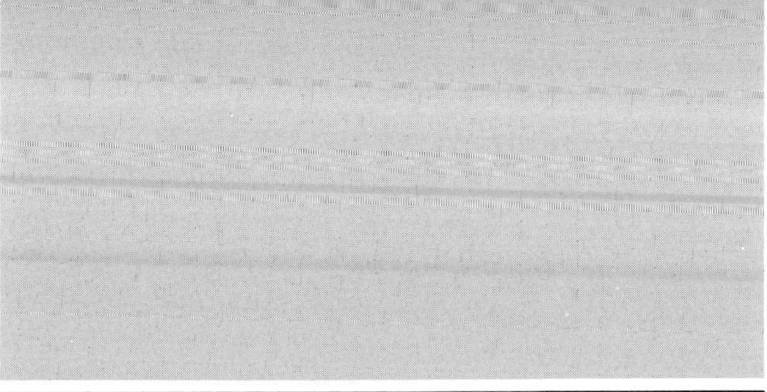

LOUIS H. HAMEL: HAVERHILL'S HORATIO ALGER

When Louis H. Hamel died in August 1975, Mayor George Katsaros ordered the flags at City Hall lowered to half staff to pay homage to the quiet, unassuming man who had contributed so much to Haverhill's development. Louis' obituary referred to his successful businesses and the many gifts his charitable foundation made to area organizations, reminders of how far he had come since his boyhood in turn-of-the-century Haverhill.

Louis was born in Exeter, New Hampshire, on August 31, 1898, the son of Haverhill natives Anthony J. and Agnes M. (Comeau) Hamel. After the family returned to Haverhill, Louis attended the Bartlett and Currier schools and peddled ice cream and candy at the city's shoe factories after school to supplement the family income. At age 14 he had obtained a work permit and a job as an errand boy in the cutting room of the Webster & Webber Shoe Company. Two years later, having acquired a thorough knowledge of the shoe-cutting trade, he moved on to the Hartman Shoe Company, where he remained until March 1916.

With the $97 he had saved from both jobs, Louis established his own company at 11 Washington Street. He was only 17 years old, but this move was destined to make him the world's largest tanner of kidskins and sheepskins.

In late 1917, Louis moved his business from the cramped confines of the 20 X 40 foot room to spacious quarters on an entire floor at 100 Washington Street. He dealt primarily in upper leathers and the cutting of shoe trimmings from remnants. In his first year, his net earnings were less than $100. By the third year he had made $25,000.

In 1920 Louis convinced his brother Arthur to go into business with him, and together they expanded the firm onto all four floors of the building. Louis purchased a small tannery in Peabody, Massachusetts, in 1921 to produce

Louis H. Hamel (1898-1975). Courtesy, Donald R. Beaton, Hamel Foundation

leather. Two years later, the growth of business forced them to move the operation to a large concrete building at 117 Essex Street. The brothers eventually took over other floors of that building, and another structure was built to fill their needs.

Louis and his brothers, Arthur, Herbert, Walter, and George, incorporated the business as the L. H. Hamel Company in 1921. Arthur was president and sales manager, Louis served as general manager and treasurer, and Herbert served as clerk. George and Walter became assistant sales manager and production processes director, respectively. By 1928 company expansion necessitated further reorganization and capitalization at $500,000. Louis and Arthur had made the company the largest producer of shoe linings in the United States.

Louis did not imitate his competitors. He created and patented his own Nu-Process system and became the leading figure in the leather industry at 36.

The company was known for its advanced management structure and had exemplary labor-management relations. In 1934 the company supported the formation of the Hamel Employees' Credit Union. Five years later the Hamel Employees' Mutual Benefit Association was founded to provide industrial and nonindustrial accident and sickness benefits and a wage stabilization plan. By 1941 the company was offering bonuses and pension plans.

Although he had only a seventh-grade education, Louis had a lifelong interest in education. In 1947 he joined a small group of Merrimack Valley businessmen who planned and developed Merrimack College. Perhaps his most enduring contribution was the establishment of the Hamel Charitable Foundation.

During World War II, Louis helped bring the Western Electric Company to the city. Always seeking to aid his fellow citizens in good times as well as bad, Louis kept the L. H. Hamel Company going despite the significant downturn in the shoe industry.

Upon his death on August 26, 1975, Louis Hamel left behind a legacy of hope and expectations. His energy, intellect, foresight, and imagination made good things happen, and his spirit lives on in the Haverhill community.

City Insurance Agency, Inc.
BANK O

CHAPTER SIX

RESTORATION, RENEWAL, AND RETROSPECTIVE

averhill's heart has always been easy to locate. The earliest generations knew it was at the place where the millstream flowed into the river, near the first meetinghouse, the burial ground, and the minister's home. By the beginning of the nineteenth century, the center had moved to the new mercantile blocks at White's Corner. One hundred years later, a third area had become the vital core of a greatly expanded industrial city. From the city hall, high school, and public library on the east side to the railroad depot on the west side, Haverhill pulsed with industrial, political, and cultural life. The midpoint of this vitality was Washington Square.

As Haverhill expanded, this extended downtown area remained the unchallenged center of the city during the first seven decades of the twentieth century. It was familiar, comfortable, and unchanging—and that was a problem. Most of the downtown buildings were of pre World War I vintage and were located on streets designed for pedestrians and limited public transportation, which benefited only those residents who lived and worked within a mile or so.

The abundance of land available on the outskirts of the

The restoration and revitalization of the Washington Street/Washington Square area served as a symbol of new hope and promise for both the downtown and the city of Haverhill as a whole. Photo by David J. Joyall, courtesy, Trustees of the Haverhill Public Library

city had attracted home builders away from the downtown area since the seventeenth century. This movement greatly accelerated in the immediate aftermath of World War II with the use of automobiles, which offered personal control over time. This factor, combined with postwar prosperity, produced a new breed of consumer: the leisure shopper.

Unfortunately, Haverhill was a prewar city with postwar needs. Downtown parking spaces were at a premium; traffic patterns on old narrow streets were a nightmare; and improvements and alternatives were called for. Parking and traffic solutions were much discussed and occasionally proposed, but nothing was actually carried out.

While words multiplied and ink flowed with suggestions on how to make Haverhill's downtown more accessible, shoppers flocked to the mecca of mobile America—the shopping mall. Since the eighteenth century, inhabitants in the peripheral parishes gravitated toward Haverhill's center for the goods that their local general stores could not provide. With the development of trolley and bus lines, the travel network expanded to include the outlying towns east and north of the city. Now, the pattern was reversed. Grocery supermarkets, upscale department stores, and flourishing specialty shops drew customers away from the older and smaller downtown stores, which gradually disappeared.

Then came the unprecedented move to the suburbs. Instead of a continuous expansion along existing streets, this shift headed toward newly built garrisons, capes, and pseudocolonial-style homes in southern New Hampshire and the small towns east of the city. The move out of the crowded, lethargic

industrial city, like the house styles chosen, implied a nostalgic attempt to recover a small-town past.

However, the exodus included a disproportionately large part of Haverhill's traditional leadership —bankers, businessmen, industrialists, professionals, and local media leaders—who moved to Atkinson and Plaistow in New Hampshire, and to Groveland, Merrimac, and Georgetown in Massachusetts. Their interest in Haverhill issues proportionately diminished.

Concern arose during the 1960s and 1970s over the difficulty of finding qualified volunteers to fill the boards of city government or participate in the annual United Fund drive. Newcomers to the city were surprised to find no active civic organizations, such as the League of Women Voters, the Men's Club, or other cultural organizations.

The disappearance of Haverhill's leadership community was soon followed by the disappearance of the city's physical center. By the late 1950s, Haverhill residents were reacting negatively to the downtown area. The majority of the downtown buildings were more than 100 years old and had not aged well, particularly in the oldest built-up section of the city, off Water Street.

Such buildings were not considered attractive or renewable for the modern 1950s and 1960s. Like the shoe industry, they were out-of-date, relics of a past that could not be recovered. The generation that grew up during World War II was attuned to the sleekness and flashiness of modern styles, which was reflected in their automobiles, furniture, and gadgets. This generation drove shiny new cars to work at Western Electric, Raytheon, and Digital. They shopped for televisions and refrigerators at enormous malls in Framingham, Peabody, and Burlington. The remaining shoe shops were relics of the past now limited to work sites for older generations or for new immigrants still learning American ways.

Washington Street in particular had fallen on hard times. Grime and time obliterated its once attractive facades and block after block was gradually converted to bars and taverns. Washington Street became an area to hurry through, eyes averted and nose blocked to screen out the smell of stale beer.

High school graduates could not wait to leave the city. Proposals for renewal, such as a new high school and new middle schools, were resisted or postponed. Too often those who resisted new construction were the same forces whose negativism had driven the giant Western Electric works across the city limit into North Andover.

So marked had apathy and unhappiness become that Dorothy Bell, president of Bradford Junior College, decided to inaugurate a business and industry seminar to focus on the city's needs. Cosponsored by the college, the Haverhill Chamber of Commerce, and the *Haverhill Gazette,* the seminar became an annual event in the 1960s, bringing together state and national figures who sought to define Haverhill's potential in a new society of superhighways and high technology.

While the seminar offered words, urban renewal offered action. According to the Slum Clearance and Urban Renewal Plan of 1958, the federal government would fund 75 percent of the costs of clearing away shabby places and replacing them with up-to-date modern buildings. This seemed ideal for Haverhill. The concept of renewal grew in popularity, and cities that adopted the concept spoke of themselves as "renaissance" cities, evoking images of life, vitality, and prosperity.

Under urban renewal a sizable parcel of land was totally cleared, and the entire site was then offered to developers. Haverhill took up the idea with enthusiasm and grand plans. The area from Mill Street to Railroad Square would be leveled as far upland as Summer and Winter streets—in effect, the entire area of the city built up 100 years before.

Phase One, the Pentucket Renewal Site, included the oldest part of the city, between Mill and Main streets. Structures to be razed included an elegant

Facing page, left and right: Federal-style buildings at the corner of Main and Water streets from the early 1880s were among those seen in the 1950s and 1960s as no longer able to serve the commercial downtown. They were demolished during the city's "slum clearance" under the urban renewal program. Photo by Bernard J. Gallagher, courtesy, Trustees of the Haverhill Public Library

Below: Although doubts about the wisdom of massive clearance had begun to surface, phase two of Haverhill's urban renewal program began with the demolition of all the buildings on the west side of Main Street above White's corner. Odd Fellows Hall was the first to go, helped by a fire in December of 1973. Photo from the Haverhill Gazette, courtesy, Trustees of the Haverhill Public Library

mansion designed by Philadelphia architect John Haviland for the Duncan family but owned since the 1890s by the Pentucket Club. The Haverhill Public Library and the Essex County Courthouse were also to be replaced by new, efficient facilities. State Highway 97 was to be rerouted above and parallel to Merrimack and Water streets.

After much debate, the first structure was razed in 1966. By 1970 a modernistic public library with long slits for windows and a Colonial-style courthouse were both perched at the corner of Main and Summer streets. Merrivista, an apartment complex for the elderly, occupied the southeastern corner of the intersection. All three buildings were constructed of red brick, but no other factor unified them.

A year later, approval was granted for a strip-style shopping center at Water and Main streets and a ten-story apartment building, with offices on the first floor, at the corner of Water and Bridge streets. The apartment building was constructed with distressed concrete in a style popularly called "Brutalistic" or "Mussolini modern." Until these last two structures went up, the area from the courthouse to Merrivista was one enormous wasteland.

Phase Two called for the clearing of the area from Main Street to Washington Square. In its place would be a climatized mall with a parking garage to meet the needs of the automobile age. A particularly appealing part of this proposal was the decision to take advantage of the riverfront to create parks and scenic walkways. In addition, at the northern end of the land, the GAR Park would be extended.

In 1974, after all of the old brick blocks on Main Street in the renewal area had been removed, the project began to change. There was to be no general clearance. The banks and the structures on the river side of Merrimack Street would not be touched, thus excluding any major use of the riverfront. The proposed parking garage would not be built at the corner of Main and Merrimack streets, and radio station WHAV would not have to be moved. An acceptable design would have to work around these exceptions before approval could be given.

The federal government began to tighten its urban renewal funding. Developers fell by the wayside, unable to raise the required financial backing. The Haverhill Housing Authority, entrusted by the government to carry out renewal, continued to initiate the systematic removal of buildings from Merrimack Street. Although the demolition of the old city hall on Main Street and the Grad Building on Merrimack Street attracted a number of opponents, complaints in general were scattered and muted. Nostalgia rather than preservation seemed the principal argument against razing.

Although Haverhill was named an "All-American City" in 1978, pessimism and depression once more affected people's attitudes. The very conditions that were to be alleviated by urban renewal were back in full force. Nothing so epitomized the frustration and sense of disaster that had befallen Haverhill as the saga of the ill-famed parking garage.

Ground breaking for the garage took place in February 1978, four years after the facility's initial planning, and was not completed for eight years. The unfinished garage became a bitter joke, and construction became a catch-22. As long as the garage was not completed, state and federal governments would not approve further work. However, without the financial assistance of the state and federal governments, no developer could carry out his plans. Haverhill was stuck with a large empty space surrounding an unusable parking garage. After years of delay, the facility was finally completed in 1986.

Residents had responded to the parking garage situation by calling for a master plan around which the city could rally. However, the calls were difficult to implement because of the lack of continuity in city government. The strong city government of the past had been replaced in 1952 with a city manager and seven councillors, with one councillor serving as a pro forma mayor. This type of government was voted out in 1965 and replaced by a strong mayor and nine councillors. However, the council candidates who favored this move were defeated at the polls except for Joseph L. Willett, the famed "stormy petrel" of midcentury Haverhill politics. All the incumbents who favored the retention of the previous type of city government were reelected.

At a time when continuous leadership was greatly needed, no mayor between 1968 and 1982 served more than two consecutive terms of two years each. Council members fared much better because Haverhill voters believed they were keeping the polls off balance by continually changing the executive while keeping an evenly balanced council.

The regular changeover in city government was paralleled by a similar insecurity of tenure for urban renewal directors. In contrast, membership on the Haverhill Housing Authority, which controlled urban renewal, tended to be long-term. By federal regulation, members served five-year renewable terms, which removed these positions from the control of local politicians. But this continuity had a negative effect in that the members tended to be committed to the total-clearance concept of urban renewal and were reluctant to consider alternative forms.

By the mid-1970s, an attractive form of alternative revitalization, the adaptive reuse of existing buildings, was proving successful and was being readily imitated. The idea was sparked in part by the nation's bicentennial celebration and led to a nationwide preservation movement that stirred local enthusiasm. A change in government regulations provided the necessary funding to implement the new concept. Instead of paying urban renewal funds directly to a citizens' group, the new system gave community development block grants to local government for general site improvement, beautification, and restoration in any area that needed upgrading.

Lewis Burton, mayor from 1976 to 1978, immediately implemented a program of preservation. Bulldozers were out, restoration was in! Haverhill native Jack Bradshaw, director of the highly regarded Newburyport Redevelopment Authority, and Jonathan Woodman, who grew up in Haverhill and was the architect responsible for many reuse plans for Newburyport's nineteenth-century red-brick buildings, were enthusiastic proselytizers.

Mayor Burton's first task was to save the Franklin Block on Merrimack Street from demolition and to open up land for a river walk. The total-clearance drive was stopped just as plans were being made to raze Washington Street. Reuse began to see results. At one end of Washington Street, The Tap rediscovered its 1930s motif and quickly became a favorite dining spot. At the other end of the street, the Judkins family agreed to restore the facade of their Pentucket Shoe Store to its turn-of-the-century appearance. These two buildings pioneered the reconstruction of Washington Street to its former vitality. The century-old Whittier Hotel underwent a face-

lift that brought back much of its charm, and when its ground floor was turned into an upscale dining room and lounge, downtown had an instant drawing card.

Probably the most exciting construction during this phase of urban renewal was the 1979 transformation of vacant shoe factories on Phoenix Row into housing for the elderly. The Phoenix Housing project was designed by Jonathan Woodman for Bethany Homes, Inc., a nonprofit organization providing affordable housing for Haverhill's older residents. The organization's previous ventures had been the newly constructed Merrivista and Mission Towers in the Water Street renewal area.

The restoration was just the tinder needed to fire up enthusiasm and hope throughout the area. Phoenix Housing was the first major project to create an awareness of the potential that lay in Haverhill's old buildings. This successful adaptation of industrial space into comfortable living quarters provided a model for other projects and also attracted permanent residents to Washington Square, some of whom had once toiled in the very buildings in which they now resided.

Phoenix Housing's location by the seawall gave its occupants a magnificent view of the Merrimack River, Haverhill's greatest visual asset. Eighteenth-century mansion builders had recognized the river's beauty and had sited their splendid homes to take full advantage of it. Commercial needs and soaring land values had prompted succeeding generations to block off the view. Now, once again, the seasonal and tidal changes of the swift-flowing waterway could be enjoyed.

A century ago, a major conflagration had destroyed old Washington Street and created a new street of Queen Anne brick and brownstone. The fire begun by the rehabilitation of the old shoe factories on Phoenix Row was one of spirit rather than flame, stripping away age-old grime and permitting new life to sprout. One by one, the old buildings in the vicinity were restored, and their elegant, long-hidden architectural designs delighted residents. Washington Street and its immediate environs once again became a place to live, work, and enjoy.

The work on the Shoe Town area was done by private investors with the aid of public money and loans from local banks. In 1983 Haverhill was selected by the U. S. Department of Housing and

Urban Development for national recognition as an example of how a city, through public and private sector partnerships, had been brought from unsightly physical decay to an area of historic character with growth potential.

Ironically, the opposite end of Merrimack Street presented a much less stirring view. As accolades were being ladled out in Washington Square, White's Corner remained a wasteland. It was not until 1986 that the parking garage was completed and construction was started on a 70,000-square-foot, four-story building to house the Pentucket Medical Associates Center.

Despite these changes, Haverhill no longer functions only around its downtown area; it has been given a new life line, Interstate 495. When the new high-speed circumferential highway was cut through the area in the 1950s and 1960s, it gave Haverhill a new artery that pumped life-giving blood back into the city. "The Platinum Pike," a phrase used by Governor John Volpe at one of Dorothy Bell's seminars, was intended to do for the outlying areas of Haverhill what Route 128 had done for Greater Boston.

The completed Interstate 495 gave Haverhill greater access to the new interstate highway system—Route 93 to the west, Route 95 to the east, thence southward to Boston and Route 128. In the past, only the railroad had tied the city so directly to Boston. The highway's placement in the city's less populated areas opened up new areas for development at minimal displacement costs. The results included industrial parks with acres of requisite parking space; new housing from single-family developments to multi-unit apartments and condominiums; shopping plazas and auto dealerships; and recreation facilities and new schools. Isaac Merrill's Haverhill had been transformed with a positive citywide impact on its industrial base, tax structure, and population.

Once again, public enterprise and public initiative cooperated, nowhere more effectively than in the efforts of the Haverhill Industrial Foundation, a nonprofit organization founded in the 1960s. It developed a creative funding system that was used to purchase land and provide seed money for incoming businesses. The results included the Newark Street Industrial Park and the immense Ward Hill Industrial Park located on Harold Rogers' Spring Hill Farm land on Ward Hill Neck.

The parks and other areas attracted a diversity of businesses from leather and shoe-related firms to chemical, technological, and research companies. The mix was typical of the general resurgence in the New England economy as it shifted from single-industry goods to broad-based products.

In 1961 Haverhill had lost the large Western Electric complex to North Andover when the city government proved unyielding to the company's request for tax abatement for its new plant. The company continued to be the chief employer of Haverhill residents. Local workers had become used to traveling to work sites outside the city. The industrial parks helped reverse that trend and attracted new residents to the housing units that were popping up everywhere. Some newcomers also became interested in the rediscovered architectural and historical treasures found in Rocks Village and Bradford, and particularly in the Victorian splendors of the Highlands and upper Main Street area.

The population drain of the midcentury was thus reversed with new blood, ideas, and enthusiasm. Haverhill was once again becoming a desirable place to live. Real estate values soared in the 1980s, much to the joy of landowners and distress of low-income families who found themselves with fewer options.

Haverhill struggled through some difficult times in the decades after World War II. The sudden hemorrhage of the Korean War took the lives of nine men. The youngest was 17-year-old Pfc. Basil W. Gewvelis; the oldest was 37-year-old 1st Lt. Joseph Matonis. Other fatalities included Pfc. John L. Brown, 19; Sgt. Carleton B. Clay, 26; Cpl. Robert C. Daignault, 19; Pfc. Phillippe L. Daigneault, 23; Capt. Joseph Januszewski, 30; Cpl. Edward F. O'Neil, 26; and Pfc. Benny Sirski, 25. More than half had lived in the neighborhood called "The Acre."

Twelve city men were killed during the Vietnam War. One casualty, Marine Lt. Brian R. O'Connor of Andover, had grown up in Bradford. The first to die, in 1966, was Pfc. Ralph T. Basiliere, 19. Cpl. Gregory C. Davis, 27, killed two days after Christmas 1971, was the last victim. Lance Cpl. Richard O. DeMaris, USMCR, 23, and S/Sgt. William L. Bonnell, 24, both killed in 1967, were neighbors on High Street in Ward Five. Other casualties included Pfc. Arthur P. Williams, 20; Sfc. James N. Finn, 36; 1st Lt. Robert B. Schena, 25; Pfc. John C. Peel, 21; Spec. 4 Barry S. Kyle, 21; Cpl.

Frederick G. Derocher, 21; Pfc. Michael J. Gambino, 19; and WO William J. Cahill, 22. At least six of the Haverhill casualties were from Ward Five.

On April 29, 1973, the Main Street bridge over the Merrimack River was renamed in memory of Pfc. Basiliere and a memorial plaque was dedicated to all Haverhill's Vietnam dead. Reverend Ernest T. Serino, a former curate at Saint Rita's church in Ward Five, captured the war weariness of the time. "I pray today that we learn to bury hatred and honor these dead by refusing war."

Already divided over urban renewal, Haverhill also found itself at odds over the war in southeast Asia. By the early 1970s, with the war entering its second decade, the cry to "Give Peace A Chance" was joined by more voices. Students from Haverhill High School, Bradford College, and Northern Essex Community College, as well as war veterans, led the peace marches that filled Washington Square and Bradford Common.

Left: This aerial photograph depicts downtown Haverhill, looking east along River Street to the hills of the East Parish. Photo by Howard W. Curtis, courtesy, Trustees of the Haverhill Public Library

Facing page: "I pray today that we learn to bury hatred and honor these dead by refusing war." With these words, the Rev. Ernest T. Serino, a former curate at St. Rita's Church, led the dedication ceremony for Haverhill's Vietnam Memorial and the Basiliere Bridge. The bridge was named in memory of PFC Ralph T. Basiliere, the first of the 13 Haverhill men to die in Vietnam. Photo from Haverhill Gazette, courtesy, Trustees of the Haverhill Public Library

The newly stirred social consciousness of the city also surfaced during the nationwide civil rights movements, even though Haverhill's black population was disproportionately small in comparison to that of other industrial cities. The 1960s and 1970s had also seen a flowering of ecumenicism among the city's traditionally separated religious groups. In the same city where Saint James High School students had silenced an anti-Catholic evangelist in the 1916 Leyden riots, and where a simplistic explanation of the local decline in the shoe industry smacked of anti-Semitism, brotherhood now bloomed. Memorial services for the Reverend Martin Luther King, Jr., and Robert F. Kennedy in 1968 carried over into multidenominational peace vigils and pulpit exchanges in the 1970s and joint action for social justice in the 1980s. Churches of all denominations provided regular meals to the hungry and built a permanent shelter for the homeless.

While the myopic in the community bemoaned the loss of the shoe industry, those with better vision applauded the way both new and long-established educational institutions improved the future of Haverhill's youth. Merrimack College in North Andover was established in 1947 for veterans and working-class youth. In 1960 Northern Essex Community College (NECCO) was created to provide low-cost public education. By offering extensive day and evening classes, both Merrimack and NECCO, which was moved to a new campus in 1970, have made higher education accessible to thousands of local residents, a large percentage of whom have been the first in their working-class families to attend college.

In 1971, Bradford Junior College, established in 1803, became a coeducational, four-year liberal arts college. After years of being a boarding school with a national and international student body, Bradford College in the 1970s turned back to its origins and once again became an active participant in the education of local students.

Haverhill Trade School had been turning out highly skilled craftsmen—electricians, printers, and auto mechanics—since 1924. After its 1973 incorporation as the new Whittier Regional Vocational Technical High School, young men and women from Haverhill and surrounding towns were offered a curriculum that addressed the needs of a service-oriented world.

From their earliest years, New Englanders recognized that open minds were more valuable than trained hands. Nature was not lavish in the resources of the land, so New Englanders found resources within themselves. The land was abundant in granite, ice, and trees. Resourcefulness turned them into cash crops. It is not coincidental that the area is synonymous with the best in education.

Haverhill is the quintessential New England city. As a survivor, it has adapted to the changes of time. This was no boomtown, destined to fade away after a brief burst of glory. Like some conservative Yankee trustee, Haverhill has carefully managed its estate so that the next generations can live well—but not too well. Recklessness and flamboyance have certainly not been Haverhill's hallmark, save perhaps for an exuberant outburst of Victoriana toward the end of the nineteenth century.

At times the city may have been too Yankee and too conservative. Of its numerous immigrant groups, no representative had made it to the top electoral spot before Irishman Albert W. Glynn became mayor in 1939. Glynn, however, was a shoeman, a staunch Republican, and a thoroughly assimilated son of Haverhill, a far cry from the Irish Democratic bosses who controlled the region's other industrial centers.

Haverhill will enter its fifth century with some enduring questions still unresolved. The tug-of-war between the downtown area and the outlying parishes continues; its most recent incarnation is between the community at large and neighborhood associations. Also unending is the debate in government between the proponents of expansion and those who preach the need for a balanced budget and fiscal restraint. Haverhill has a history of change in appearance, economy, and population, yet each era has produced spokesmen who want to indefinitely preserve the present or return to a nostalgia-tinted past.

Perhaps Haverhill has also been too reluctant to change, too willing to make do, use up, and wear out when in fact the occasion called for a new set of clothes. Yet, the city by the Merrimack continues at a sedate pace, adapting and surviving. But just when it lulls you with its unchanging step . . . it suddenly dances!

THE VALHOULI BROTHERS

Greece suffered much during World War II. First, the Italians invaded in 1940. One year later, the intensity of local opposition prompted the Germans to rescue their Axis ally. The Germans drove the Greek royal government into exile and established an army of occupation. An active resistance movement arose.

Amid the turmoil, Nicholas Valhouli, mayor of a provincial capital in Macedonia, was arrested and imprisoned. His wife and five young sons, ranging in age from 11-year-old twins Jon and Peter to infant Dimitri (James), took refuge with her parents in a small village. Jon Valhouli remembered the challenge of walking alone for two days to visit his imprisoned father, fighting back the fear induced by endless childhood tales of wild dogs and wolves. The 11-year-old's courage was needed by the entire family to survive these desparate times.

After a lingering illness, Nicholas died in prison. Shortly after, the British invaded Greece in 1944 and drove the Germans from the country. The right-wing royal government was restored to power by the British, even though the resistance movement had demanded a democratic government. European peace was immediately succeeded by civil war in Greece, which did not end until 1949.

With peace, however, came a large-scale emigration. Jon and Peter, now 20, accompanied by their mother and brothers Michael, 18, Archimedes, 14, and Dimitri, 9, came to Haverhill in 1951. Their uncle, George Valhouli, owned the flourishing Lincoln Shoe Company. The older boys got jobs at the shoe factory, and the younger two pursued the education that had been postponed by the war.

The Lincoln Shoe Company did not promise a long-term future, so the younger brothers were encouraged to continue their education. The other brothers would find work that provided both independence and income. The solution was to enter the rapidly growing service industry of hair styling. Jon went to Boston to learn this new trade, courtesy of the G.I. Bill of Rights, and returned to Haverhill in 1958 to open his own shop. Peter and Michael joined him soon after.

By working 12-hour days and six-day weeks, the men were able to design and build their own shop on South Main Street in Bradford in 1971. They had also seen their younger brothers through college and graduate work. Archimedes (Midi) became a Certified Public Accountant, and Jim was pursuing a career as a college professor after earning a Ph.D. in literature. The classic immigrant ethic of hard work and education had once again paid off.

Like their predecessors and others still to come, the Valhouli brothers have maintained their heritage while pursuing the American Dream. The language, religion, and culture of their native country are kept alive in their American-born families, and the Greek ebullience is displayed at family gatherings as members and friends join in exuberant folk dances of their native land.

The Valhoulis' American side emerges through their participation in the service industries of hair styling, accounting, and education. Their integration is reflected by their places of business. Jon joined Haverhill's building preservation and renewal movement when he opened a shop in 1976 on the site of the old fire station in Groveland center, an area that was once part of Bradford. Following his brother's example, Midi purchased the classic 1836 Greek Revival Pearl House, which faces the Common in Bradford. That building had most recently served as a branch library.

Thus, the durable past continues to merge with the vitality of the present, an age-old story of Haverhill that does not wear with re-telling.

The five Valhouli brothers and their widowed mother were photographed in July of 1951, the year they left Greece. Courtesy, James N. Valhouli

CHAPTER SEVEN

PARTNERS IN PROGRESS

T he institutions whose histories are profiled in the following pages provide a good sampling of the many types of businesses in the Haverhill area. Some are old, beginning here in the nineteenth century, and some are very new, moving to the area during this decade. Some serve an international constituency while some limit their activities to the local area. Some are branches of large, national concerns, but most were founded here and have roots deep in local soil. Many are multigeneration firms, while others are the creation of the present chief executive officer.

Within the obvious diversity found among these organizations, there has emerged a strong, shared point of view among their leaders that is important to note. All are committed to community service. The record is very clear—schools, churches, hospitals, libraries, and United Fund agencies, as well as the city itself—all have been and are today beneficiaries of thousands of volunteer service hours and hundreds of thousands of dollars given to improve the quality of life in the Haverhill area.

These business leaders also share a pride in their city and an abiding interest in its heritage. They value its architecture, taking particular pleasure in its distinguished nineteenth-century buildings. They value its literary tradition as exemplified by the poet, John Greenleaf Whittier. They understand the worth of its location and the remarkable resources of its natural setting—its lakes and parklands, its proximity to the seashore and the mountains, as well as to the urban riches of Boston.

They value this place. They are committed to it. They are investing themselves here and are proud of their decision to do so. With pride in the past, deeply engaged in the present, they are individuals whose eyes are set upon the future. And, they see good things there.

The organizations whose stories are related here have chosen to support this important literary and civic project. They illustrate the variety of ways in which individuals and their businesses have contributed to the Haverhill area's growth and development, making it an excellent place to live and work.

Haverhill became a city in 1870, and a Common Council was elected to oversee the city's affairs, formerly handled by town selectmen. The first Common Council included, seated left to right: Daniel Fitts, C.P. Messer, William A. Brooks, Moses How, M.G.J. Emery, G.W. Wentworth, and Edward B. Bishop. Those standing are, left to right: William L. Bass, B.F. Leighton, R.B. Jaques, J. Kendell Jenness, Calvin Smith, and J.F. West. Courtesy, Trustees of the Haverhill Public Library

BRADFORD COLLEGE

Bradford College, founded in 1803, is a four-year, independent, coeducational liberal arts college with an enrollment of more than 400 students from across the United States and throughout the world. Its 184-year history is the chronicle of an institution that has continuously evolved to meet changing educational and societal needs while maintaining its commitment to the primacy of the liberal arts. Today Bradford remains on the cutting edge, nationally recognized as a trailblazer for American higher education.

The college began as Bradford Academy, one of New England's earliest coeducational schools. Prominent citizens of the city's parish established the school "for the purpose of promoting piety, religion, and morality, and for the education of youth in . . . the liberal arts and sciences . . ." The founding meeting was in Kimball Tavern, a historic landmark adjacent to Bradford Common that is still an important part of the college's living history.

Bradford Academy attracted students from all over New England and the world. Its early graduates took rigorous liberal arts courses of study that prepared them for positions of leadership in early nineteenth-century society. They became teachers, lawyers, doctors, clergymen, and missionaries. As these graduates fanned out across an expanding American frontier, the school's reputation grew.

Life was changing in nineteenth-century America. Educational opportunities became more plentiful with the rise of the common school. However, these opportunities were not equally distributed among all the nation's youth. Accordingly, in 1836 Bradford chose to devote itself exclusively to the education of women—one of the earliest American schools to do so.

Listed in the National Register of Historic Places, Academy Hall was completed in 1870. The Bradford College Alumni Association, one of the oldest in the nation, was formed at its dedication.

Under the influence of Abigail Hasseltine, the academic program grew more rigorous. At a time when education for women usually meant little more than instruction in the social graces, Bradford women studied metaphysics, Latin, surveying, and celestial mechanics. Although these courses seem esoteric by today's standards, in their day they were distinctly practical. The curriculum reflected the skills and knowledge expected of the trained missionary, nurse, schoolteacher, and landholder. Throughout the rest of the century Bradford continued to add advanced courses to its curriculum.

By 1932 Bradford had completed the transition from a secondary school to a college. That year Bradford Academy became Bradford Junior College, the first such institution to be accredited by the New England Association of Schools and Colleges.

By the spring of 1971 the college was ready to embark upon another major step. It opened its enrollment once again to male students, and for the first time in nearly 140 years Bradford men took their places in the classroom beside the young women. Later that year the institution received authorization from the Commonwealth of Massachusetts to grant the bachelor's degree and change its name to Bradford College.

In 1982 Arthur Levine became president of Bradford College, and the institution made a commitment to the Bradford Plan for a practical liberal arts education, a program that combines Bradford's historic tradition of quality liberal arts education with a desire to prepare students for life and for careers.

Professor John Roberts conducts a class in the Samuel K. Robert Computer Center.

GREATER HAVERHILL CHAMBER OF COMMERCE

CHAMBER MISSION STATEMENT

The thrust of your chamber is to organize and focus on the energies of those who believe that a community worth living in is a community worth improving.

It is the vision of the Greater Haverhill Chamber of Commerce that our area become identified as a fresh, wholesome, and concerned region where our badge is a conspicuous cleanness, inspired by the coming together of all people and all places of business. We pledge the resources of your Greater Haverhill Chamber of Commerce as a catalyst to bring about an exciting new image for the benefit of everyone.

May 1983

On April 11, 1888, a board of trade was organized in Haverhill. Its objectives were to unite the " . . . energies and influence of our citizens for more effectual production and promotion of the public welfare of the City of Haverhill and to act in the development of all legitimate enterprise which would tend to increase its prosperity."

In 1916 the board of trade changed its name to the Haverhill Chamber of Commerce. The annual dinner that year was well attended, and the organization's rallying cry was "Keep Haverhill Clean! Today, Tomorrow, and Everyday!"

Today known as the Greater Haverhill Chamber of Commerce, the organization unites the enthusiasm and commitment of business people from the seven Massachusetts and eight New Hampshire communities that comprise the greater Haverhill area. The more than 550 member firms are dedicated to "organizing and focusing on the energies of those who believe that a community worth living in is a community worth improving."

As part of this thrust the cham-ber has put major effort in a program called Clean Commitment—the vision that the area can become identified as a fresh, wholesome, and concerned region "where our badge is a conspicuous cleanness, inspired by the coming together of all people and all places of business." The chamber is pledged to bringing about an exciting new image for the benefit of everyone.

The organization encourages businesses to get to know each other and to do business with each other through Business After Hours gatherings, Business to Business breakfasts, the Business Bulletin, and an annual Business-Community Exposition. The regional nature of the chamber is emphasized through all its programming and also through meetings outside Haverhill, such as recent meetings in Plaistow and Merrimac. Greater Haverhill is a market area with a commonality of interest.

Building partnerships is also a prime goal. Cooperative efforts with government at all levels are extensive. The medical community, nonprofit organizations, schools and colleges, and the arts community are all finding the chamber an ally. Founded in April 1984, the Greater Haverhill Chamber of Commerce Community Arts Foundation is an excellent example of a new chamber/arts partnership benefiting the entire area.

The association is concerned with building the internal and external image of the city and the area. There is a clear understanding of the importance of attitude, self-concept, and above all a sense of pride. Haverhill and its surrounding area have many assets. Rich in history and natural beauty, located near Boston yet close to beaches and the lakes and skiing of New Hampshire, Haverhill has fine schools, including two colleges and many recreational opportunities within its boundaries. It is a good place to live.

It also has an exceptionally skilled work force, a strong work ethic, rich ethnic diversity, and varied and affordable housing and industrial space well located near major interstate highways.

The Greater Haverhill Chamber of Commerce believes that these assets should give the area a sense of pride, and is committed to building people's pride in themselves, their achievements, and their community. This is the mission the chamber has had for the area for 100 years. It is as important and fresh today as it was when the organization was founded in 1888.

The Whittier Building, home of the Greater Haverhill Chamber of Commerce.

YOUNGBLOOD PLUMBING AND HEATING COMPANY, INC.
YOUNGBLOOD MECHANICAL CONTRACTORS, INC.

When Frank Youngblood and his firm were profiled in *The Moen Mixer,* the organ of Moen, a division of Stanadyne Corporation, in 1975, he was termed "Haverhill's Southern Yankee."

Youngblood grew up in the red clay hills of Georgia near a hamlet called Woodstock, not far from Atlanta. He came of a farming family—and if it had not been for World War II, he might never have heard of Haverhill, Massachusetts.

During the war Youngblood was assigned for a while to Camp Edwards on Cape Cod with a coastal artillery outfit. One night he met a young lady named Ruth Franklin at a church-sponsored dance at the base.

After his discharge and putting in one crop on his father's farm in the spring of 1946, Youngblood decided to head back to the Merrimack Valley. He and Ruth Franklin were married later that year, and Youngblood went to work for Western Electric.

The firm went out on a long strike, and Youngblood's father-in-

Frank Youngblood (right) receiving the Just Cup as National Contractor of the Year at the National Plumbing, Heating, and Cooling Convention in 1972.

law, Harry Franklin, asked him to come work in his thriving plumbing shop and use the G.I. Bill for his on-the-job training. He picked up the tools of the trade in 1947, and has never laid them down.

Following Franklin's death in 1953 Youngblood moved on to the Haverhill Oil Company, continuing his plumber apprenticeship training. He got his journeyman rating in 1956 and his master's ticket two years later. Early in 1959 he took the big step he had been planning ahead for, and struck out on his own.

He started out in his own garage at home—with his tools and a pickup truck. As the business grew, a succession of locations around Haverhill followed, and Youngblood started building his team. One of the original

Frank Youngblood and his son, David, confer with a customer by telephone from Youngblood's office. Visible are many of the professional and civic awards won by Youngblood.

crew was Jerry Viens, now head estimator. His 25 years of service at Youngblood attests to the success of the companies' philosophy, which emphasizes increasing the skills of workers in a merit shop and an open-door policy to all employees.

The business has always been a family affair. For 25 years Ruth Youngblood was a full partner serving as full-charge bookkeeper, office manager, and customer relations chief. She recently retired from daily participation in the office to devote more time to tennis and volunteer activities. Her duties are now ably carried out by Paula Fay-Staples and Wendy O'Donohue with the help of a computer.

The Youngbloods' son, David, is also a part of the team. He got his first work permit at the age of 14 and has worked his way up in the firm. David has a son Tyler who hopefully will be a part of the business in the future. In addition to earning his master's ticket, he has handled purchasing and pricing duties, served as general manager, and is currently vice-president and chief operating officer. This allows Frank Youngblood to slow down a little and devote time to his responsibilities in state and national professional organizations.

From one man and a pickup, the Youngblood companies—whose focus is major industrial and commercial applications—have grown to an annual volume of approximately $4 million. They are recognized leaders in the field of plumbing, heating, and cooling contractors in central New England.

The companies' designers and engineers are responsible for the heating, plumbing, and cooling systems of many of the new-as-tomorrow structures that have risen in the area. Fifteen teams and 15 vehicles are on the job at any given time.

These mobile units are supported by an excellent home-base staff, located in the companies' headquarters at 32 Ashland Street. The reception area, containing photographs of recent Youngblood projects, leads to administrative offices, a conference room, and the computer center. There is also an employee lunchroom, a warehouse, and truck bays.

Frank Youngblood has earned the respect and recognition of his adopted community through his commitment, service, and involvement in both industry and nonbusiness activities. Within the trade he has served in all the chairs of the Haverhill Master Plumbers' Association, and has continued as state director for 18 years. Other offices include the presidency of the Massachusetts Association of Plumbing, Heating, and Cooling Contractors and national director, in 1984, of the National Association of Plumbing, Heating, and Cooling Contractors.

In 1972 he was elected to the highest recognition the National Association of Plumbing, Heating, and Cooling Contractors can bestow: the

national Contractor of the Year Award. He had won this same honor in the Merrimack Valley in 1970, and in 1985 was elected Massachusetts Contractor of the Year. At the 1987 Massachusetts Plumbing, Heating, and Cooling Convention, Youngblood was presented with the Bradford Rose Award, its highest honor.

Youngblood has served as superintendent of Sunday school at the First Baptist Church of Haverhill for 30 years. He and Mrs. Youngblood were drawn together originally in part by their church activities, and they have remained devoutly involved ever since. Youngblood received the initial award for outstanding service from the Greater Haverhill Council of Churches in 1960, and a little later the B'nai B'rith annual award for service to the community. During his tenure as chairman of the board of the local Salvation Army unit, Youngblood led the drive to build the organization's building. He is also active in committee work for the YMCA, and has served as a director. This is a community interest he and his son share: They are a rare father-son team on the Haverhill YMCA's board.

Youngblood was a longtime member of the Haverhill Lions Club, serving 11 years as chaplain, and a member and past director of the Greater Haverhill Chamber of Commerce. He has also been deeply involved with the Merrimack Valley United Fund as the area chief for the plumbing/heating trade.

As Youngblood becomes less active in the daily affairs of the companies he founded, he gives more of his time to education. He was the first chairman of the advisory board at the Whittier Vo-Tech school, and is currently a trustee of the Merit Shop Institute—an organization concerned with apprenticeship training—of the Associated Builders

One of the many large office complexes in the greater Boston area with plumbing, heating, and cooling systems by Youngblood.

and Contractors, Incorporated.

Frank Youngblood can be proud of his record of achievement and service. However, the entrepreneur spends little time reviewing the past. "As I reflect on more than a quarter-century of business, I have to say that any business should really not ever look back on past accomplishments, but look ahead to the future. At Youngblood Plumbing and Heating Company, Inc., and Youngblood Mechanical Contractors, Inc., we believe in looking ahead, keeping abreast of the latest technologies, and meeting the challenges of the 1980s. We are committed to our pledge of a quarter-century ago: to provide the best in quality work and service for our builders."

Management and office duties are carried out by (left to right) Wendy O'Donohue, Jerry Vines, Frank Youngblood, Paula Fay-Staples, and David Youngblood.

CEDARDALE, INCORPORATED

In the September 1986 issue of *Club Industry,* the business magazine for fitness and racquet club management, the cover story was about "an industry legend—it is one of the largest, most talked about, most envied, and most highly regarded clubs in the country." The club under discussion was Cedardale.

Each year more than 100 club owners come to visit Cedardale Athletic Club to see it for themselves and get some sound business advice from its owners. What they see is a facility covering 13 acres in the Ward Hill section of Haverhill. Five acres are devoted to outdoor fun with 5 pools, 10 tennis courts, and 2 pavilions, one with a food and beverage service, all highlighted by the spectacular water slide. Inside the massive building complex are the traditional facilities: basketball, tennis, and racquetball courts; a fitness and aerobics center; pool; saunas; steam rooms; whirlpools; a nursery; and lounges. Additional amenities include a travel agent, physical therapist, and pro shop.

All of this began in the late 1960s, when Dale and Olive Mae Dibble built an outdoor club in Groveland, Massachusetts. On 14.5 acres of land they built a 50-meter pool and four outdoor tennis courts.

With more than 7,500 members, some of whom drive 50 miles to use this exceptional facility, Cedardale is a legend in the health club industry.

Five acres devoted to outdoor fun include 5 pools, 10 tennis courts, and 2 pavilions, all highlighted by a spectacular water slide.

Ten years later Dale teamed up with Clif George and Ed and Zoe Veasey to form Cedardale, Incorporated. In 1971 Cedardale opened. It was a family affair. Zoe and Olive Mae would record the club's financial statistics in a leather-bound ledger. The 31,320-square-foot club grossed $168,000 per year.

Today Cedardale is a 175,000-square-foot club grossing in excess of $4.6 million per year—four times the industry average, and with a profit margin that is the envy of the industry. The growth and profitability have been due to a remarkable combination of extremely careful bookkeeping, dedication to building an outstanding management team, and commitment to providing the best in equipment and facilities.

The highly qualified and talented management team share in all aspects of the business. In addition to being conversant with the club's financial status, managers vote on all decisions through regular meetings and share in the club's profits. The Cedardale management style is as successful as its bookkeeping practices.

Cedardale's commitment to quality in facilities and equipment is evident immediately. In a newly renovated area are two aerobic rooms with special floors created by a Scandinavian firm, allowing each section of the floor to respond to the body exercising on it; a 90-pound girl exercising next to a 200-pound man will feel no effect from the man's weight on the floor. The increased responsiveness of the floor also helps prevent shin splints and other exercise-related injuries.

In the same area is a 2,000-square-foot, fully equipped physical therapy center with state-of-the-art equipment. Staffed by two physical therapists, the center treats 170 patients weekly and offers Cedardale members free introductory consultations.

Cedardale continues to renovate and change; keeping abreast of the newest and best in the industry is a constant challenge that the facility meets head on.

With more than 7,500 members, some of whom drive 50 miles to use this exceptional facility, Cedardale is a vibrant, exciting club—and an enhancement of life in the Haverhill area.

NEFOR ENGINEERING AND MANUFACTURING COMPANY, INC.
NOFSKER COMPONENT PRODUCTS, INC.

Nefor Engineering and Manufacturing Company, Inc., is engaged in the manufacture of precision metal products. The business was founded in 1954 in Cambridge, Massachusetts, by Frederick Pais, who headed the company as president until his retirement in 1982. William Nofsker joined the firm in 1970 as vice-president of sales. He began concentrating on sales to the then-emerging high-technology industries of New England. After Pais' retirement, Nofsker became president.

By 1979 Nefor Engineering and Manufacturing was in need of expansion space unavailable in Cambridge. Many firms were relocating to escape the state's tax policies, and locating in relatively undeveloped areas where land was cheap and highway access easy. However, Nofsker decided to stay in Massachusetts; with the oil crisis at its peak, he chose to locate in an urban environment to lessen commuting for the employees.

In August 1981 Nefor and its entire manufacturing operation moved to the former Hamel Leather factories on Essex Street in Haverhill. They were the largest reinforced concrete buildings in the world when they were erected early in the century. The company occupies 30,000 square feet of space in what is now known as the Burgess-Lang Tech

William J. Nofsker, president.

Robert Pais (right), in charge of manufacturing, with quality-control inspector John Cunha.

Center. Employing approximately 50 people, Nefor produces precision sheet-metal fabrications, assemblies, and machine parts for a large number of high-tech firms in the area.

Nofsker and Robert Pais, who is responsible for manufacturing, feel strongly that people are the most important ingredient in a company. "We are constantly seeking more experienced and trainable people. Firms like ours hope to provide a suitable bridge of employment opportunities from the shoe-related industries of the past to the high-tech industries of the present and future."

The second firm, Nofsker Component Products, Inc., is a multi-person manufacturer's sales agency founded by William Nofsker in 1969. Nofsker Component Products, Inc., specializes in the sale of custom mechanical components to the New England industrial market. During the early years the company operated from a small office in Sherborn, Massachusetts. In 1974 the firm moved to Cambridge. Seven years later Nofsker Components moved to Haverhill along with Nefor Engineering and Manufacturing.

Nofsker Components provides

The Nofsker Component Products team.

sales engineering and marketing services for Nefor Engineering and other companies engaged in custom manufacturing. The common thread linking Nefor Engineering and Manufacturing Company, Inc., and Nofsker Component Products, Inc., is William J. Nofsker. He is an excellent example of the businessman drawn to Haverhill by its affordable factory space, its location, and its work force. Bill Nofsker came for the usual reasons but he then found himself caught up in the architecture and history of the place. His firms occupy Haverhill's most important twentieth-century industrial buildings, the last and largest construction projects of the local shoe industry. He and his companies have revitalized the buildings and are a source of employment opportunity for the area's workers. Bill Nofsker is using Haverhill's past to build Haverhill's future. He and his firms are outstanding representatives of Haverhill's new industrial development.

The historical Burgess-Lang Tech Center, headquarters of Nefor Engineering and Manufacturing Company, Inc., and Notsker Component Products, Inc., was once the home of Hamel Leather Enterprises, which played a significant part in Haverhill's early history.

FREDERICK E. MALCOLM INSURANCE AGENCY, INC.

Haverhill native Fred Malcolm opened his insurance business in 1946. He was just out of the Marine Corps, and the venture was a one-man firm operating out of his house. By 1948 it had grown to half an office in the Haverhill National Bank Building, and Malcolm's wife, Marilyn, worked each afternoon so that he could make calls.

Malcolm had worked in the home office of Liberty Mutual, where he met his wife, while a student at Boston University. Upon completion of his degree, the firm offered him a permanent job, but he and Marilyn chose to return to Haverhill.

In 1965 Malcolm purchased his present building, a Victorian town house at 185 Main Street, adjacent to city hall, and restored it to meet his business needs. His son, Fred Malcolm, Jr., joined the operation in 1975, after graduating from Northeastern University. Today they head a firm of seven full-time and four part-time employees, providing all forms of insurance—property, casualty, and life.

Fred Malcolm is a quietly eloquent man who can tell you very clearly what he wanted for himself and his family. He wanted to be a part of his home city; his definition of being a part is to participate, to invest oneself in the affairs of the community. The entrepreneur has certainly done that, and his son is continuing the role.

The history of Malcolm Insurance, therefore, is the story of a man, his family, and the services they provide to the people of the Haverhill area. Of course, the business services are important, but what sets the Malcolms apart is the civic involvement they feel to be a part of "doing business."

Chairman of the All-America City effort when Haverhill won the title in national competition in 1979,

The Malcolms demonstrate pedestrian safety to kindergarten children at Sacred Hearts School in Bradford, a community service program that won them national recognition in 1983.

Malcolm is also a former president of the Community Chest, the Greater Haverhill Chamber of Commerce, and the Greater Haverhill Foundation, which has been instrumental in developing an industrial park and bringing new industry to the city.

In 1983 the Malcolm agency won national recognition. It received the Public Communicator of the Year Award from its professional organization, Professional Insurance Agent, for a unique program on pedestrian safety that father and son provide for area kindergartens.

Born of Malcolm's concern with the high incidence of pedestrian traffic accidents involving small children, the program uses a fleet of colorfully painted miniature vehicles, one-eighth scale, including a fire truck, a pickup truck, a Model T, and a sleek racer, to illustrate pedes-

trian safety rules for youngsters on the school grounds, following a classroom presentation.

"My son and I probably repeat 'Look both ways' 200 times during a session. The kids may get sick of hearing it—but when the program is over, we hope they will instinctively remember to look both ways whenever they cross a street," says Malcolm.

The children who successfully pass their safety lesson receive a bright green "I am a Safe Pedestrian" button and are given an information packet to take home to their parents. They also receive a ride in one of the miniature cars.

This program is just one vivid example of the Malcolm commitment to public service. The sign on the building housing Frederick E. Malcolm Insurance Agency, Inc., says it well: "Personable Insurance." Says its founder, "We want to emphasize that our firm provides a high level of service. We give time to our people." Fred Malcolm and his family have provided not only insurance but also inspiring civic leadership to Haverhill for more than 40 years.

THE HAVERHILL CO-OPERATIVE BANK

On August 13, 1877, the Haverhill Co-operative Savings Fund and Loan Association was organized in Nathan Longfellow's real estate office at the corner of Merrimack and Fleet streets. Amos W. Downing was president; John W. Tilton, secretary; and J. George S. Little, treasurer. There were 12 directors. Seven days later the commissioner of banks gave his official approval, and the second-oldest cooperative bank in the Commonwealth was born.

In the early years the association members met monthly, the first meeting being held in Good Templar's Hall at 53 Merrimack Street. The first loan was made to F.S. McKinney, to whom the sum of $400 was sold at auction at a premium of 20 cents a share.

Attorney Willard G. Cogswell explained how the bank functioned in the early years on the occasion of the institution's 65th anniversary in 1942:

"In those early days all members of the association attended the monthly meetings, paid their dues, listened to reports, and then departed. Thereupon the officers put up to auction the money collected as dues, and would-be borrowers bid what we should now call usurious premiums for their loans. McKinney, for instance, actually received only 80 percent of his $400, which notwithstanding he had to pay back in full with interest at 6 percent. It was very good business indeed—for nonborrowing shareholders!"

In 1887 Haverhill Co-operative engaged rooms in the Dagget Building, which it shared with Page Insurance. William H. Page, the grand old man of the bank, was its secretary, and it had become usual to do bank business out of the office of the secretary. In 1895 space was leased from the Haverhill National Bank. Through all these changes, and indeed well into the middle of the twentieth century, a Page remained as secretary. In fact, three generations of Pages have been associated with the institution: William H. Page, secretary and treasurer from 1878 to 1916; his son, James G. Page, who succeeded him and served until 1947; and James R. Page, the third generation, appointed president in 1960.

The bank has prospered and grown steadily over the years. In 1963 the Citizens Co-operative Bank merged with Haverhill Co-operative, followed in 1982 by The Whittier Co-operative Bank. In 1978 the institution occupied its new quarters at 180 Merrimack Street, overlooking the river—owning its own building for the first time in its 100-year history.

Today The Haverhill Co-operative Bank is headed by Thomas Faulkner, named president and treasurer in 1980 to succeed Albert J. Ingham. Active in civic affairs, Faulkner heads a 110-year-old institution that has evolved into a $75-million concern. The Haverhill Co-operative Bank is an outstanding example of its type, a creation of local people to meet local needs. It has proved a sound instrument. It has survived several depressions, including the Great Depression of 1929, and the hectic years of World Wars I and II. During all those ups and downs, not one person lost so much as one dollar in savings in this or any other cooperative bank in the state, and mortgage foreclosures were held to a minimum because the bank knew its clients and could deal with each case on an individual basis.

"We're a Haverhill bank serving Haverhill people," Faulkner explains. "Our depositors live here and our loans are made here. That allows us to really know our customers." The Haverhill Co-operative Bank is proud to be a part of the community, prospering with the people it serves.

Organized in 1877 as the Haverhill Co-operative Savings Fund and Loan Association, the institution has been serving the Haverhill area from various locations since that time. Today The Haverhill Co-operative Bank is headquartered in this modern facility at 180 Merrimack Street.

The board of directors of The Haverhill Co-operative Bank in 1987 are (seated, left to right) J. Leo Ouellette, Nicholas Peterson, Thomas R. Faulkner, and John E. Callahan. Nancy A. Paszko is in the center and in the back row (left to right) are Norman J. Shepherd, Richard M. Blustein, Malcolm D. Kimball, Hartley R. Cranton, H. Louis Farmer, Burt J. Barrett, and Henry T. DiBurro.

KENOZA VENDING CO., INC.

Kenoza Vending Co., Inc., was founded in 1947 by John Der Bogosian after he acquired a confectionery store on Kenoza Avenue in Haverhill. His parents and brother Edward contributed much to the business in the beginning.

In 1948 another brother, Hy Der Bogosian, began in the vending aspect of the business. In addition to the pistachio and nut machines that had come with the confectionery store, the brothers had begun to satisfy the demand for sandwiches and related food items. At first their mother made the sandwiches, which she wrapped in waxed paper. What didn't sell was discarded at the end of each day.

Since 1962 Kenoza Vending Co., Inc., has been on West Main Street in Merrimac, Massachusetts. From this base 27 employees using 13 vehicles provide a complete foodvending service to some 100 firms for food and 150 for coffee services from Route 128 on the south to Portsmouth, New Hampshire, on the north and as far west as Lowell.

Kenoza Vending Co. provides a wide variety of beverages, snacks, and food items in the most modern vending machines. Whether freshly brewed coffee, yogurt, a submarine sandwich, or a blueberry muffin is desired, Kenoza will provide it.

The ability to provide such a wide variety of food and beverage items in perfect condition is the result of careful attention to finding and keeping the best supplies, cou-

The company provides a wide variety of beverages, snacks, and food items in the most modern vending machines to industries, schools, and offices in eastern Massachusetts and southern New Hampshire.

pled with the most modern and efficient operations at the Merrimac base. Products are stored at optimum temperature while on site, and a minimum of time elapses between a product leaving the supplier and its arrival in a customer's vending machine.

The efficient and courteous mobile personnel provide 24-hour maintenance service using modern, completely equipped service trucks that have telephone communication with the Merrimac office. The staff not only provides fresh food products for vending but also keeps the machines in perfect condition.

The Kenoza Vending Co., Inc., staff and fleet of service vehicles at the West Main Street facility in Merrimac.

The Merrimac base is staffed by the three Der Bogosian brothers and a dedicated staff who keep the entire operation meeting its goal of providing the very best in service, maintenance, and personal attention to all its customers, while offering quality food-service products at a reasonable price.

The firm provides coffee, cold drinks, milk, a wide variety of sandwiches, candy, pastry, and ice cream. In addition to vending machines it also supplies bill changers, radar ovens, office coffee equipment, and condiment counters.

The Der Bogosian brothers' business has grown from a small confectionery store to a 16,000-square-foot plant with 500 square feet of refrigerated area, servicing a fleet of 13 vehicles. The firm even supplies attendants for three customer locations, each of which serves some 300 people.

Today Kenoza Vending Co., Inc., provides complete automatic cafeteria service from its building on West Main Street in Merrimac to industries, schools, and offices in eastern Massachusetts and southern New Hampshire. The business has grown dramatically since 1947, but the quality of the product and the personal concern of the Der Bogosian brothers and their staff are still the same as in those first days when their mother made the sandwiches.

FALCONE PIANO COMPANY

Santi Falcone immigrated to Somerville, Massachusetts, from Mazzarino, a small town in the Caltanissetta province of central Sicily, when he was 14 years old. His love of music was nurtured by his father, who had an untutored but memorable tenor voice. When Falcone completed junior high school, his father decided the boy's voice was good enough to merit formal training and sent him overseas to the Santa Cecilia Conservatory in Rome. There, one afternoon, Falcone wandered into one of the school's recital halls and watched an elderly blind piano tuner at work. He became fascinated by the skillful work of the tuner and maneuvered himself into a position as the man's apprentice. The experience left an indelible mark on the boy.

His father died when Falcone was 17, and he returned to the Boston area to help the family. The youth sought every opportunity to work on pianos. He was soon hired by the Boston Conservatory of Music to maintain all its pianos, and in the evening he served a growing private clientele.

In 1971, after a tour of duty in Vietnam with the Army, Falcone came home with about $13,000 saved from his pay. He opened the New England Piano and Organ Company, a small retail store on Main Street in Waltham, Massachusetts. Within five years the entrepreneur was selling pianos and organs from seven outlets in New England, with 45 employees and revenues of $2 million. Falcone had, by that time, repaired or rebuilt at least one model of every important piano in the world. Determining he could build better, and for less money, he sold off all but one of his stores and began a four-year period of research and development. Gradually he mastered the details of manufacturing, and the first Falcone piano was born in the summer of 1982.

Today the 42-year-old craftsman produces three sizes of grand pianos (none smaller than six foot, one inch) in a six-story converted furniture factory in Haverhill. He and his 60 employees handcraft, slowly and very carefully, each piano to the specifications of Falcone—and tailored to the buyer. "The piano should be an extension of the artist," says Falcone. This personal tailoring of the instrument to the buyer is the reason Falcone pianos are never sold through dealers.

The Falcone piano is not what the average family buys. It is in the same market as Steinway and Baldwin, and its natural habitat is the stage of a concert hall or the studio of a professional musician.

Falcone has set out to make the best piano in the world—and many believe he is doing just that. When Rudolf Serkin dropped by to try the piano in 1983, he admits he went to encourage "an amateur." After playing for about a half-hour, the maestro rose from his chair, clasped Falcone's face in his hands, and said, "Mr. Falcone, *you* are the artist."

Falcone moved his business to

Santi Falcone, chairman and founder.

Haverhill in 1986 because it had all the advantages of location his firm needed to grow: appropriate space at reasonable rates, good transportation, and a fine labor pool. Each month production grows in the Haverhill facility. Beginning with only four in July 1986, Falcone hopes to increase his production to 835 pianos per year, employing 100 workers. This will come with time, however. It takes time and great care to make the best piano in the world.

Santi Falcone with David Page, technician.

HAVERHILL PAPERBOARD

In 1902 four men moved from Indiana to New England looking for an industrial site. Martin Williams, Crawford Fairbanks, William J. Alford, and W.S. Lowe, in a reversal of the industrial trend of that and later days, came east and found what they were seeking on the banks of the Merrimack River in Bradford. On their 48-acre site the four began construction of the present mill, forming a corporation called the Haverhill Boxboards Company that began operations on January 2, 1903.

In 1920 the Haverhill Boxboards Company plant was purchased along with several others by Robert Gair Company, Inc., of New York. A major merger of the period, the consolidation began the growth of an organization that became a leader in the production and distribution of boxboard and other paper products.

Robert Gair was a pioneer in the paper goods industry. Born in Scotland, he came to the United States at age 13. A soldier in the Civil War, he was mustered out as a captain. He then entered the paper business in New York. He sold paper in almost every form from hoopskirts to oyster fry boxes. But it was Gair's pioneering in box production that made his fortune. He invented cutting and creasing cartons in a single operation and also developed corrugated board by combining three sheets of paper.

The 1920 merger with Haverhill Boxboards Company was part of Gair's move to gain control of the production of folding cartons, paperboard, corrugated, and solid fiber shipping containers nationally. Haverhill Boxboards became part of a chain of mills stretching across the eastern United States and Canada.

In 1956 the Haverhill mill was acquired by Continental Can Company from Robert Gair Company, Inc., and subsequently sold in June 1971 to become a division of Newark Boxboard. The mill is now operated as Haverhill Paperboard; yet despite the corporate changes over the years, the mill is still known and referred to in Haverhill as the "Boxboards."

Although converting wastepaper into boxboard had been going on at the Haverhill site since 1902, it is a little-known process. The production process first involves receiving and classifying the various grades of wastepaper. The wastepaper is then mixed with water in large tubs, processed through a series of cleaners and refiners, and pumped to the two paper machines for formation into a paper web. The web is pressed, dried, then slit and cut into rolls or sheets for delivery to the customer. Although the basic process has remained unchanged over the years, modernization of methods and equipment have more than tripled the daily output of the paper machines.

In the mid-1960s there was a national awakening of interest in conservation and recycling, and Haverhill Paperboard became a hero among factories, turning tons of wastepaper into usable products. This was nothing new for the firm since wastepaper had always been its raw material; but in the 1960s it was a newly valued activity.

The late 1960s was a difficult time for the firm. The boxboard industry in the East suffered from overcapacity and a weak economy, and stream and air pollution became national issues. The Merrimack River was being called the Ganges of the East, and all sources of river pollution were under attack. Haverhill Paperboard used river water in its operations and returned water to the river. The mill had located there in order to do just that. The recycling hero had fallen from grace.

The plant was scheduled for closing when Newark Boxboard purchased it in 1971. Newark invested several million dollars to modernize the manufacturing process and bring the mill into complete compliance with the clean air and water regulations. This investment, coupled with the cooperation and efforts of the employees, provided a turnaround that once again made the mill a profitable, growing operation.

Today Haverhill Paperboard remains a part of the Newark firm, one of the largest independent producers of boxboard in the United States. Headquartered in New Jersey, this privately held company has 12 paper machines located from California to Massachusetts. Each plant operates on a decentralized basis. Haverhill is a separate profit center responsible for its own sales, manufacturing, and financial functions. However, the corporate umbrella protects the individually run plants from regional business fluctuations.

During the 1950s and 1960s fully 95 percent of all the paper cigar boxes used to package cigars were manufactured at the Haverhill mill. This operation was phased out in the 1970s due to competition from the "five pack" folding carton used to package the cigars.

Today most of the Haverhill plant's production is used within the New England and New York regions. The product is shipped to plants that convert the boxboard into paper matches, game boards, shoe boxes, pizza boxes, and a host of other packaging products that are used by consumers throughout the United States.

Currently Haverhill Paperboard operates 24 hours a day, 6 days a week and produces 310 tons of paper a day on two paper machines. It employs 200 people. The plant uses some 80,000 tons of wastepaper each year, which is collected from offices, supermarkets, factories, and community recycling programs throughout the New England area. The majority of this waste would end up in landfills were it not used as a raw material to produce boxboard.

Haverhill Paperboard has a remarkable history of employee benefits and loyalty. In 1947 the *Haverhill Gazette* ran a feature story on the mill. At that time three of the employees had been with the firm since 1905, one since 1906, and three since 1907. An additional 45 employees had 25 or more years of service.

The situation is similar today. There are still many employees with more than 20 years of continuous service. Through the years there has been a history of cooperation and exceptional relations between management and the employees. The company continues its original policy of local hiring, steady employment, and excellent wages and benefits.

Through 84 years of doing business, under four different corporate managements, Haverhill Paperboard remains a major employer in the city, weathering both world wars and economic cycles, producing a quality product from wastepaper, and providing a good place to work for hundreds of local people.

Though methods have changed over the years and much of the hand labor necessary during the era of these photographs has been replaced by sophisticated machinery, the end product, boxboard and other paper products, is still the same at Haverhill Paperboard.

THE FAMILY MUTUAL SAVINGS BANK

Founded in 1828 as the Institution for Savings in Haverhill and Its Vicinity, Family Mutual was the ninth savings bank to be established in Massachusetts. James Duncan, a leading businessman, called together a group of Haverhill's most respected citizens and proposed that they "provide a means by which our people will be encouraged to save and practice thrift."

The first bank location, a tiny office with a safe, was situated on Main Street and was open to receive deposits each Wednesday from 9 a.m. to 12 p.m. only. The *Essex Gazette* reported on the first day of the bank's operation: "The number of depositors who appeared ... exceeded the most sanguine expectations. Among them were persons from 8 or 10 to 60 years of age, and of various conditions of life, depositing sums of three dollars and upwards." Deposits could be made by persons residing in the towns of Haverhill, Methuen, Bradford, Boxford, Andover, and Amesbury, Massachusetts, and Plaistow, Atkinson, and Salem, New Hampshire. Withdrawals were more complicated than they are today. Money could be withdrawn only on the third Wednesday of each month and after one month's notice had been given to the treasurer.

The town's leading citizens were involved in the bank, among them Isaac How and Benjamin Greenleaf, who served as the first vice-presidents, and James Duncan, who served as president until 1835 when he was succeeded by Rufus Longley, who served until 1841 and again from 1843 to 1851. The other presidents were Charles Minot, 1841; John A. Appleton, 1851; George A. Kimball, 1883; Woodbury Noyes, 1892; Elbridge G. Wood, 1894; William W. Spaulding, 1910; Fred D. McGregor, 1929; Alfred E. Collins, 1939; Harry R. Davis, 1941; Lawrence J. Ewing, 1949; Stanwood D. Evans, 1964; and Donald K. Laing, 1973 to present.

The bank moved in 1883 to a store in Masonic Temple, sharing quarters there with the Haverhill National Bank until 1895, when it moved to its present location at Merrimack and West streets.

Quite early the Institution for Savings changed its lengthy title to the simpler Haverhill Savings Bank, and in 1968 it again changed its name to reflect its original goal of serving Haverhill and its vicinity. It became The Family Mutual Savings Bank, the name it retains today.

From a handful of deposits in 1828 Family Mutual grew to 2,350 depositors and $424,721.36 in deposits by 1853. At the end of 1986 there were 63,977 savings accounts, and the bank's assets totaled $337.8 million.

A local bank founded by local people to serve the local area, The Family Mutual Savings Bank has always been characterized by a friendly and helpful spirit. It is also an institution that has been able and willing to change with the times to provide safety and a fair return to its depositors and an increasing range of banking services to the community.

Family Mutual provides banking services with its nine bank offices, of which five are located in Haverhill in addition to offices in the towns of Groveland, Topsfield, Middleton, and Boxford. In June 1987 the bank opened a 10th office in Georgetown. The institution also operates and provides mortgage services through its recently opened mortgage center in Haverhill. In addition to a full range of deposit banking services, it also provides a full range of lending programs, including mortgages, commercial loans, and various types of consumer credit. The bank also is involved in equity participation and joint ventures and is a major resource for local construction financing.

Much of this growth has been made possible by Family Bank's most recent change. In 1986 it converted from a mutual to a stock financial institution. This process, completed in November 1986, produced an enthusiastic response on the part of depositors, employees, and directors, and provided the bank with more than $30 million of capital to strengthen the bank and provide resources for additional community investment.

With this change The Family Mutual Savings Bank still retains its local commitment. As president Donald Laing put it, "We have always positioned ourselves as a community resource, staffed by local people and providing needed financial services in the local community."

The Family Mutual Savings Bank, headquartered at 153 Merrimack Street, serves Haverhill and vicinity with five bank offices in Haverhill as well as offices in Groveland, Topsfield, Middleton, Boxford, and Georgetown.

NORTHERN ESSEX COMMUNITY COLLEGE

Founded in 1961, Northern Essex Community College has continued to provide high-quality, affordable education and training to the growing population of the Merrimack Valley for more than 25 years. The college offers a comprehensive curriculum, meeting the needs of those who plan to transfer to senior colleges or universities; seek occupational training and certification of job competency for careers in business, industry, the allied health fields, or service occupations; need increased exposure to fundamental skills areas; or wish to study at the college level as part-time students for credit or personal enrichment.

The college is constantly developing and adapting its curriculum to respond to the educational, social, and training needs of the community—its citizens, its business and industry, its human service agencies, and its public and private institutions. Recognizing that for a community college the concept of "community" is as vital as the term "college," the institution also provides a wide range of cultural and recreational activities open to all residents of the Merrimack Valley.

Northern Essex Community College first opened its doors in the fall of 1961 to 186 students, most of whom came from Haverhill and the communities immediately adjacent. Lacking land or buildings of their own, the college faculty met students in a former elementary school.

President of the new school was Harold Bentley, a Congregational minister who left the active ministry in 1944 to join the faculty at Worcester Junior College. He later became president, a post he filled until accepting his appointment at Northern Essex Community College. Bentley was responsible to the Massachusetts Board of Regional Community Colleges, but a local advisory board composed of civic and business leaders helped shape the distinct character of the community college.

The new institution quickly outgrew the small school and additional space was found in the city's former high school, in church basements, and in a grange hall. Meanwhile, plans for a permanent campus were adopted, and in 1971 nearly 2,000 students were enjoying the benefits of a 106-acre campus near Kenoza Lake, only a stone's throw from Interstate 495.

When Bentley retired in 1975, he was succeeded by John R. Dimitry, a native of Detroit whose professional career has been spent in community college teaching and administration. Under Dimitry's leadership the curriculum and enrollment at NECC developed and expanded in the occupational and technical program area; nearly 70 percent of today's student body is enrolled in professional and

Students enjoy the beauty of Northern Essex Community College's Haverhill campus in the spring.

career programs. Programs of community service were expanded, a Center for Business and Industry was established at the college to better meet the needs of local business and industry, and cooperative education programs were instituted and began to flourish.

In 1981 new legislation provided for a Board of Regents to oversee all public institutions of higher learning in the Commonwealth. Each institution is managed by an 11-member local board of trustees that includes representatives from alumni and the student body.

Northern Essex, the largest community college in Massachusetts, currently serves 9,600 students from nearly four dozen communities stretching from Lowell to Newburyport in the Merrimack Valley, employs 917 faculty and staff members, and has satellite facilities in Lawrence, Andover, Dracut, and Newburyport.

The Massachusetts Board of Regents recently recommended that Northern Essex Community College be given $11 million for a permanent, comprehensive campus in Lawrence, a plan that has been approved by the governor but must still be passed by the state legislators.

Located on the shores of Lake Kenoza, Northern Essex Community College serves 9,600 students from nearly four dozen communities stretching from Lowell to Newburyport.

SHEEHAN AND SCHIAVONI

Sheehan and Schiavoni continue a long and distinguished legal tradition in Haverhill. Currently the firm is composed of Richard J. Sheehan, Jr., Timothy T. Schiavoni, Anthony Cogswell serving as of counsel, and several associates.

Anthony Cogswell's father, Willard Goodrich Cogswell, began the tradition in 1939 when, after having been associated with attorneys Tilton and Sawyer, he founded the law firm of Cogswell, Davis and Soroka. W. Clifford McDonald and John S. MacDougall, Jr., later were associated with the firm before going on to serve as judges.

Upon graduation from law school in 1973, Richard J. Sheehan, Jr., became associated with the firm of McDonald, Cogswell, MacDougall, Gleed and Laraba. In 1976 he became a partner with Anthony Cogswell in the firm of Cogswell, Laraba and Sheehan.

Early in the 1950s Theodore L. Schiavoni began the practice of law in Haverhill. He later associated with Alfred J. Cirome and Michael Mooradian.

Timothy J. Schiavoni, a nephew of the late Theodore L. Schiavoni, worked with his uncle throughout law school and associated with the firm in 1973. Five years later Schiavoni became a partner in the firm of Schiavoni, Cirome and Mooradian.

Friends during the course of their early practice, Sheehan and Schiavoni formed a partnership on January 1, 1986. As part of their initial planning, they began the design and construction of their present law office, located at 70 Bailey Boulevard. The strikingly post-modern structure, which was the first privately funded project in the urban-renewal area since 1979, is located on the site of an early Schiavoni home.

Sheehan and Schiavoni is a full-service, general practice law firm. It

This modern building, the first privately funded project in the urban-renewal area of Haverhill since 1979, houses the law firm of Sheehan and Schiavoni. It is located on the site of an early Schiavoni family home.

has developed a strong practice in the field of commercial law and real estate, with particular emphasis in representing banks and local developers active in the commercial and industrial growth of the greater Haverhill area. Its client base is local, regional, and, at times, national in scope. The firm has significant capabilities in real estate development and conveyancing, financing, commercial transactions, estate planning, and probate.

The firm also participates in pro bono programs servicing the less fortunate throughout the Merrimack Valley. This is a reflection of the personal commitment of both Sheehan and Schiavoni to public service and involvement in the community.

Born in Haverhill and educated at Boston College and Albany Law School of Union University, Richard J. Sheehan, Jr., has held numerous positions of responsibility in local organizations, including the Greater Haverhill Chamber of Commerce; the Greater Haverhill Foundation; Haverhill Community Development Corporation; Trustee of the Haver-

hill Public Library; Northern Essex Community Mental Health Services, Inc.; BayBank Merrimack Valley, N.A., board of directors; The First National Bank of Boston Regional Advisory Board; The Family Mutual Savings Bank Board of Incorporators; and active involvement in St. Joseph's Parish and school.

Timothy J. Schiavoni was born in Haverhill and educated at Cornell University, University of Villanova School of Law, and Suffolk University School of Law. In 1974 he was elected to the Haverhill School Board for a two-year term. He has acted as counsel for and has served on many local boards, including Lone Tree Council Boy Scouts of America; Haverhill Chapter of the American Cancer Society; Northeast Cultural Arts Center, Inc.; the Greater Haverhill Community Arts Foundation; and the Greater Haverhill Chamber of Commerce. He has served on both the board of incorporators and the board of trustees of the Pentucket Five Cents Savings Bank and is actively involved with the Sacred Hearts Parish and school.

Sheehan and Schiavoni combine private practice with public service. Their wide involvement in, and knowledge of, the greater Haverhill area serve both their clients and the community well.

C. FRANK LINNEHAN & SON FUNERAL SERVICE

The C. Frank Linnehan & Son Funeral Service was founded in 1930 by C. Frank Linnehan and is presently owned and operated by his only son, John J. Linnehan. The firm has grown and expanded over the past half-century, and the Linnehan family has been very involved in local and regional affairs and has done much to prepare Haverhill to meet the challenges of the twenty-first century.

C. Frank Linnehan, a Haverhill native, was educated at St. James High School and Boston College. He owned and operated the Linnehan Transportation Company with terminals in Haverhill and Boston. The original location of C. Frank Linnehan & Son was 20 White Street. In 1941 the firm moved to its present location, 129 Kenoza Avenue. In 1983 the company expanded to meet the growing needs of its clients and purchased the Noonan Funeral Home, 52 Salem Street, Bradford.

John J. Linnehan is a graduate of Haverhill High School and Tufts University. He met John F. Kennedy in the early 1950s and worked in Kennedy's 1958 reelection campaign to the U.S. Senate. Linnehan also worked for Kennedy during his 1960 presidential campaign. He aided the Kennedy campaign in New Hampshire and Maryland primaries and was a delegate to the Democratic National Convention that nominated Kennedy. Following the nomination, Linnehan ran Kennedy's campaign in New York State.

President Kennedy appointed John J. Linnehan as the Assistant Administrator for Congressional Affairs of the U.S. Small Business Administration (SBA). While he was with the SBA, Linnehan brought the Local Development Loan Program to Haverhill. This was an innovative plan for the economic development of cities that had only been used in Alabama and Minnesota prior to its use in Haverhill. The program resulted in the creation of the Greater Haverhill Foundation and the development of the Ward Hill Industrial Park.

In 1966 President Lyndon B. Johnson appointed Linnehan as chairman of the New England Regional Commission. This commission was made up of the six New England governors and Linnehan, who served as the representative for the federal government. The commission was established by the Public Works Act of 1965 and was created to foster economic development.

Beginning in 1960 John Linnehan was actively involved with the Massachusetts and New England congressional delegation members in Washington. For 15 years he was a political adviser and campaign treasurer for the Speaker of the House of Representatives, Thomas P. O'Neill, Jr. In 1968 he was director of scheduling for the vice-presidential campaign of U.S. Senator Edmund S. Muskie, who later was U.S. Secretary of State. Linne-

John J. Linnehan, current owner and operator of C. Frank Linnehan & Son Funeral Service.

han also served as the finance committee chairman for Congressman Peter W. Rodino, Jr., chairman of the House Judiciary Committee.

Linnehan has been a guest lecturer on the federal government and federal legislation at several colleges and universities, including Boston College, Tufts University, Simmons College, Clemson University, University of Lowell, and Northern Essex Community College. He has been actively involved in business seminars for banks, national trade and professional associations, and development groups.

John Linnehan was the founder of the Suburban National Bank of Arlington and serves as vice-president and is a member of the Board of Directors. He also owns a real estate development company in Haverhill.

After 14 years in Washington John J. Linnehan returned to Haverhill in 1973 and assumed roles in his national and state professional associations and maintained his political activities. He has been active in many civic and municipal organizations, including being a board member of the Greater Haverhill Foundation, Inc., president of the Greater Haverhill Chamber of Commerce, chairman of the Occupational Advisory Council of Northern Essex Community College, chairman of the Harry M. Pettybridge Charitable Trust, and president of the Catholic Charities of the Merrimack Valley.

John Linnehan has accomplished much for his native city and these accomplishments have been recognized, most recently by the Haverhill Fire Fighters, the Haverhill Bar Association, and the Haverhill High School Student Council. Through the high quality of his business, his political concerns, and his community activities, Linnehan continues to work for the betterment of the city of Haverhill.

PHILLIPS, GERSTEIN, HOLBER, LaFLAMME, MIGLIORI & BARRON

Phillips, Gerstein, Holber, La-Flamme, Migliori & Barron's history begins with its founder, Herbert P. Phillips, a Haverhill native. He grew up in the city where his father headed the oldest leased department in Mitchell's Department Store on Merrimack Street. Educated in city schools, Phillips graduated from Bowdoin College and Boston University School of Law and has been a member of the Massachusetts Bar since 1957.

In 1962 Phillips left Goldman & Curtis, the Lowell firm with which he was associated, to establish a practice in Haverhill. Between 1962 and 1976 Phillips headed a succession of partnerships that evolved into the present firm in January 1984. Presently comprised of 13 attorneys and more than 30 support staff, it is the Merrimack Valley's largest full-service law firm—serving businesses and individuals from its offices in Massachusetts, New Hampshire, and Maine. Although it also practices in Florida and New York, most of the firm's attorneys were either born or have lived in the Haverhill area all their lives, lending a strong local base to the firm's practice of law. The firm presently offers its clients legal experience in all phases of the law.

The firm's growth has been constant since 1976 and continues in

Herbert P. Phillips, founder.

several areas of law, including estate and financial planning, litigation, personal injury, real estate, and tax law. The firm's original offices were in a small suite on the first floor of 25 Kenoza Avenue, Haverhill. As the practice increased in size it expanded to a portion of the second floor. It now occupies the entire building, with the exception of a small suite on the first floor, and in 1987 extensive renovations were made to provide an efficient and enjoyable working environment for its professional and clerical personnel.

The firm's attorneys represent a wide range of specialties and backgrounds. Michael A. Gerstein, a native of the Lawrence-Andover area whose family was prominent in the clothing business for many years, and Stuart M. Holber, a Haverhill native and a member of three bars (Massachusetts, New Hampshire, and Maine), along with Phillips, lecture extensively at community colleges in the areas of tax and business law, are frequent participants in seminars, and have all held responsible community posts. Phillips was Haverhill City Solicitor in 1978-1979.

Gerard R. LaFlamme, Jr., Michael J. Migliori, and Daniel T. Chabot were classmates at Haverhill High School. LaFlamme, a former high school track star, specializes in litigation, and Chabot, who returned

to his native city from his former employment with a Boston law firm, specializes in personal injury law. Migliori is president of the Haverhill School Committee and, with wife Karen L. Fiorello, forms a rare husband/wife legal team. Fiorello specializes in domestic relations, while her husband is an expert in zoning and environmental matters pertaining to businesses and real estate developers.

In 1984 the firm of Gleed and Barron merged with the firm. Gleed and Barron gave strength in real estate, commercial transactions, banking, and probate law. Gleed brought with him more than 100 years of title abstracts dating back to the firm of Soroka, Cogswell, McDougall and McDonald.

The newer associates, George A. Karambelas, Robyn Lee Frye, and Timothy H. Barnes, have strengths in general practice that aid the balance of the firm. While Karambelas and Frye as Haverhill natives reaffirm local ties, Barnes brings New York connections to the firm.

The success of the firm reflects a commitment to practicing law in a responsive, thoughtful, and intelligent fashion. The firm and the lawyers within are committed to their clients and to serving them well. They extend that commitment to the community not only in their participation in Haverhill events, but also in their sponsorship of joint efforts for education and community development.

Of counsel is Vinson W. Grad, a former prominent local businessman whose area of specialty is securities law. The support staff is headed by Barbara Leone Maglio, who has been with Phillips for 25 years.

Whatever one's need in legal matters, the firm of Phillips, Gerstein, Holber, LaFlamme, Migliori & Barron can provide outstanding service.

Herbert P. Phillips (seated) with fellow partners in the law firm (from left, standing) Gerard R. LaFlamme, Jr., Michael J. Migliori, William J. Barron, Michael A. Gerstein, and Stuart M. Holber.

COMPUGRAPHIC CORPORATION

Today words are an integral part of daily life. They are everywhere you go, everywhere you turn and, chances are, Compugraphic Corporation played a part in creating them.

Compugraphic was founded in 1960 in a storefront in Brookline, Massachusetts, the vision of its co-founders, William Garth and Ellis Hanson, who sought to apply computer technologies to the typesetting process. Throughout its history Compugraphic has carried on this vision and has led the way in applying increasingly more sophisticated technologies to the photocomposition and typesetting process. Most recently the company has addressed operations such as integrating photographs and artwork with typeset text, automated publishing, and plain-paper output.

Compugraphic is a member of the Bayer family of companies, which includes Mobay Corporation; Miles Laboratories; Agfa-Gevaert, Inc.; Helena Chemical; and Deerfield Urethane.

Since 1975 Compugraphic Corporation has been headed by Carl E. Dantas, president and chief executive officer. Headquartered in Wilmington, Massachusetts, Compugraphic employs more than 4,000 people who work in seven facilities situated along Interstate Routes 93 and 495, in field locations nationwide, as well as in wholly owned subsidiaries in Canada and Mexico, and a type distribution center in Ireland. Nearly 500 of these employees work in the manufacturing facility located within Haverhill's Ward Hill Industrial Park. Ground was broken for a 102,000-square-foot building in Haverhill in 1978.

Compugraphic products are used in the creation of newspapers, books, magazines, advertisements, and many corporate documents. Although newspapers and commer-

This artist's rendering shows Compugraphic Corporation's Haverhill manufacturing facility on a rise above Exit 48 on Interstate 495 in the Ward Hill Industrial Park.

cial operations have been the firm's traditional customers, businesses, federal government agencies, educational institutions, and trade organizations also use Compugraphic equipment in their in-house graphics, printing, and technical publication departments.

A pioneer in the development of this corporate publishing marketplace, Compugraphic's ability to offer complete systems was a key to its early development of this market. Today the EditWriter®, introduced in 1977, and the Modular Composition System, released in 1981, represent the most successful products in the industry's history.

Because customers require a broad range of high-quality typefaces, Compugraphic established its Typo Division in 1970. Then, as now, the division was dedicated to the design, production, and marketing of type. Today Compugraphic has the largest library of typefaces and the largest type design facility in the world. The Font Technologies Division, created in 1986, adapts, manu-

factures, and markets this type for electronic printing and desk-top publishing applications.

In addition to equipment and type products, the Accessories and Supplies Division provides a full selection of type-related products and consumable supplies used in the graphic arts industry.

Innovation, versatility, quality, reliability, and support are all words used to describe Compugraphic Corporation. For more than a quarter-century Compugraphic has achieved success by defining and meeting customers' needs through superior composition and typesetting systems and products.

This selection of Compugraphic typefaces illustrates how the creative use of typography can help to convey thoughts, moods, and feelings.

POPE MACHINERY, INC.

In 1920 Lyman B. Pope established a business to provide maintenance for shoe machinery. He soon began to design and produce a range of machinery for making wooden heels for ladies' shoes. In the early 1940s Pope took the heart of his shoe machinery, the spindle, and developed it. Pope's spindles could be used on machines for milling, grinding, boring, and turning. He was the first to offer a component to fit in machines being built by other machine tool shops.

The Pope spindles were sold nationwide. Pope motored from state to state in the early years introducing his products. Soon they were in every toolroom and service facility across the country and even went abroad with lend-lease during World War II. By the 1950s Pope Machinery was mass producing a limited range of spindles. However, more and more customers were coming to the firm and saying, "I have a special job. Can you make this for me?" As a result, the company was evolving into the production of specialized and high-precision spindles.

By 1979 Pope Machinery was an internationally known business with a product range of considerable depth and variety. Lyman Pope was 78 years old and decided to sell his business to a British company, Brammer PLC. Peter Clay, who has headed Pope Machinery since the Brammer purchase, says, "We were interested in expanding into the United States and felt the acquisition of Pope offered an excellent opportunity."

Today Pope Machinery has a 100-page catalog and offers some 22,000 design options. The firm also continues to excel in the design and production of custom spindles. "And, of course, Pope now makes a 'smart spindle,'" explains Nathaniel Sawyer, who has been with the firm since 1950. "Today, as assembly lines become more automated, the spindle must have sensor components."

In addition to the building on River Street, which was expanded in 1962, Pope now has service centers at four locations in the United States—the Detroit Service Center, 1981, Cincinnati Center, 1982, Boston, 1983, and Newport Beach, California, 1984—and three in Europe. "The centers give our customers immediate response to any problems they are having in the field," says Sawyer.

Pope's 75 employees design and produce a remarkable range of spindles for a diversified list of customers. In addition to a wide variety of spindles for the automotive industry, the firm also produces spindles for such high-technology customers as Raytheon, AT&T, General Electric, Polaroid, Kodak, Gillette, and such government installations as the Portsmouth Naval Yard. To satisfy the special demands of the electronic industry, Pope makes a spindle that uses tiny drills (twice the diameter of a hair) with rotational accuracy of .00001. Perhaps the biggest spindle was for Du Pont, weighing in at 2,000 pounds.

Pope Machinery, Inc., continues to grow. In 1983 the firm bought Precision Rotor, an English company that makes air bearing spindles. Now known as Pope Precision Rotor, the company's product offers infinite accuracy for such tasks as drilling circuit boards. The firm is thriving under the leadership of its British owners, but Peter Clay is quick to point out that all the recent growth is based on Pope's tradition of quality and a staff that has been with the organization for years. "There are several families that have put 40 years into the company. There are fathers and sons, brothers and sisters, who have worked here for many years." It is their skill and Lyman Pope's idea that over the past 67 years has made Pope Machinery, Inc., a synonym for quality in the worldwide machine tool field.

An aerial photo of Pope Machinery, Inc., taken on March 30, 1946.

OGDEN MARTIN SYSTEMS, INC.

Ogden Martin Systems, Inc., a wholly owned subsidiary of Ogden Corporation, was formed in April 1983, when Ogden entered into a co-operation agreement with Martin GmbH of Munich, West Germany. Ogden Martin Systems and its subsidiaries market, design, finance, engineer, construct, start-up, test, operate, maintain, manage, and, in some cases, own resource recovery plants. These facilities generate electricity and/or steam that is sold to the local utility or a nearby industrial customer. Ogden Martin's plants range in size from 300 to 3,000 tons per day (TPD).

As of mid-1987 the Martin technology was scheduled to be used in more than 130 plants either under construction or in operation worldwide. Since 1983 Ogden Martin Systems has been selected to design, construct, and operate 20 plants throughout the United States. The company has three operating facilities, 7 under construction, and approximately 15 others in various stages of development. When completed these facilities will serve more than 8 million people nationwide.

Under construction since January 1987, the Haverhill Resource Recovery Facility represents a three-way partnership between Haverhill, Lawrence, and Ogden Martin Systems. Unlike many other municipalities throughout the country, the two towns already had an existing facility in operation since 1984. It was, however, experiencing frequent maintenance problems and faced the danger of becoming financially insolvent.

The existing refuse-derived fuel facility (RDF) was owned by Refuse Fuels Associates—a limited partnership organized in 1982 under the laws of the Commonwealth of Massachusetts. The general partner of RFA is Refuse Fuels, Inc., a corporation organized in 1978 under the laws of the Commonwealth of Massachusetts. Refuse Fuels, Inc., was owned by various local individuals.

Scheduled for completion in early 1989, the Haverhill Resource Recovery Facility, the first Ogden Martin facility in Massachusetts, will provide 1.3 million residents of the Lawrence/Haverhill area with an efficient solution to solid waste disposal.

The RDF facility, located in Lawrence, currently provides 11 megawatts for sale to the Massachusetts Wholesale Electric Company and 5 megawatts, as well as 60,000 pounds of steam per hour, to an industrial park.

In October 1986 Ogden Martin Systems of Haverhill offered to operate and retrofit the existing RDF facility and associated assets, provide a zero-interest loan for needed disposal trucks, and finance a new mass-burn facility.

The 1,650-TPD Haverhill Resource Recovery Project represents the first Ogden Martin facility to be located in Massachusetts. Comprised of two 825-TPD units, the plant will provide the towns of Lawrence and Haverhill with efficient service for the next 20 years.

The new plant will generate approximately 35 megawatts of electricity that will then be sold to New England Power Company and provide approximately 1.3 million residents—representing 15 towns—with an efficient solution to solid waste disposal. It will be completed in early 1989.

ANTHONY-BROOKS INSURANCE AGENCY, INCORPORATED

Anthony-Brooks Insurance Agency began in 1919, when Ernest F. Brooks opened an insurance office in Haverhill. Nine years later Phillips Brooks joined his father in the operation.

In 1932 Frederic Anthony returned to his native Haverhill from Connecticut, where he had learned the insurance business, and set up a desk in the waiting room of the office of his father, Dr. Francis W. Anthony, at 81 Merrimack Street. He was joined by his son, Richard S. Anthony, in 1939.

The two firms merged in 1964 to create the Anthony-Brooks Insurance Agency. Donald Anthony, a member of the third generation, entered the firm in 1973.

Today the company, which in 1986 moved to brand-new, expanded offices on South Central Street in Bradford, is headed by Richard S. Anthony with his son, Donald, as vice-president. Their staff of six includes Margaret Allen, who has been with the firm for 35 years; Gloria Godbout, a member for 33 years; and Dorothy Credit, who has been a full-time employee for 16 years following a period of part-time service in the 1950s. Three newer employees include Joyce Smith, Linda Giangregorio, and Beth White O'Connor, head of the new financial

The staff of Anthony-Brooks Insurance greets you with a smile.

New, expanded offices on South Central Street in Bradford were occupied by Anthony-Brooks Insurance Agency, Incorporated, in 1986.

planning division.

Together the staff provides 158 years of combined experience to clients. The agency also offers the latest in services and the most advanced technology. All services are computerized, which provides instantaneous access to a client's records for speed and convenience of service. In addition, the agency has direct computer communication with The Travelers, enabling it to write a policy immediately. Anthony-Brooks has been using computers for 12 years, the first agency in town to do so.

Anthony-Brooks has always provided unique services for its clients, such as a licensed, on-site staff person to inspect auto accident damage. In addition, it issues the check to pay for repairs immediately—eliminating the usual wait for insurance company approval.

Now Anthony-Brooks is pioneering in a new area, free financial planning. Clients who are interested in individual and group retirement plans, disability income protection, group health insurance, and a variety of personal investment options can get the information they need from Anthony-Brooks. This new service to both individual and business clients continues the firm's tradition of providing "insurance as we would like to buy it."

Richard and Donald Anthony believe that their agency is successful because it is a team effort on the part of every member of the staff. "We really share," said the younger partner. This father-and-son team also shares generously in the activities of the city and of their profession. Both are Eagle Scouts heavily involved in scouting. Richard has been active in the civic endeavor for 50 years, and is currently president of the Lone Tree Council Boy Scouts of America. The two men are members of the Greater Haverhill Chamber of Commerce and officers of the Elmwood Cemetery Association, to name a few of the groups that benefit from their services. They also are members of a number of professional organizations and have served on producers' councils for The Travelers and Commercial Union Insurance Companies, representing the views of independent agents to the management of these large corporations.

Anthony-Brooks Insurance Agency, Incorporated, is proud of its 70-year history of providing affordable insurance and efficient service to its clients. The personal attention of its veteran staff is combined with the support of the latest technology and information to provide the best solution for the client's insurance and financial planning needs.

MacGREGOR, SPURLING, HART AND TRAKIMAS ESQUIRES

The law firm of MacGregor, Spurling, Hart and Trakimas Esquires was founded in 1922 by Allan B. MacGregor, who opened an office at 47 Merrimack Street at the corner of Fleet.

In 1951 A. Bruce MacGregor joined the firm. This father-and-son partnership remained on Merrimack Street until 1971 when, relocated by urban renewal, the practice moved to 105 Kenoza Avenue. This handsome classical revival house, which has recently undergone complete refurbishment, is still headquarters for the firm, now numbering four partners.

In 1977 Dennis Spurling and Michael Hart of Haverhill joined the firm, and in 1984 Robert Trakimas became the fourth partner. Trakimas is a trial lawyer from Winchester who handles all litigation for the firm's clients.

MacGregor, Spurling, Hart and Trakimas, one of the oldest law firms in the city, is a general practice with an emphasis on real estate law and work for local corporations. It has the largest library of real estate title abstracts in the city, containing more than 15,000 different titles for real estate located throughout the Merrimack Valley.

The practice has a long relationship with the Family Mutual Savings Bank. In 1941 Allan B. MacGregor became counsel to the Haverhill Savings Bank, forerunner of Family Mutual, a position he held until 1959. He was succeeded by his son, who continues to hold that position today. The senior MacGregor served as a trustee until 1970, a role also held by his son who is now a director.

Community involvement was a hallmark of MacGregor, Spurling, Hart and Trakimas from the beginning. Allan B. MacGregor served two terms in the Massachusetts legislature in the 1920s and was also active in local affairs. He was president of

(From left) Michael J. Hart; Robert G. Trakimas; A. Bruce MacGregor, son of the founder; and Dennis M. Spurling are partners in one of the oldest law firms in Haverhill.

the Morris Plan Bank, Union Mission, and the Pentucket Club, as well as treasurer of the Whittier Club.

A. Bruce MacGregor has been a director of the George Wadleigh Home for Aged Men, Inc., the Visiting Nurse Association of Haverhill, and the YMCA; a councillor of the Haverhill Historical Society; chairman of the Cancer Fund Drive; and president of the Haverhill Bar Association. Also active in the Unitarian Universalist Church in Haverhill, he serves as treasurer of the first parish, chairman of the board of trustees, and member of the Permanent Fund Committee. He has been chairman of the Merrimac Planning Board and a member of the Merrimac Finance Committee and the Board of Appeals.

Dennis Spurling has been involved in Boy Scouts of America in Haverhill for eight years and has served as president of Lone Tree Council. He also served for two years as president of the YMCA, with which he has been involved for 10 years. Spurling has served as a director of the Haverhill Visiting Nurse Association and as chairman of the Greater Haverhill Heart Fund. Twice a member of the Board of Selectmen of Atkinson, New Hampshire, he has also been a member of Atkinson's Conservation Committee.

Michael Hart is active in the Democratic party in Haverhill. He is currently chairman of the Democratic City Committee and has also served as its treasurer, working in various political campaigns on behalf of party candidates. He is a former corporator of the Family Mutual Savings Bank and served two years as president of the Haverhill Chapter of the American Cancer Society. Hart is also a new member of the board of directors for Emmaus, Inc.

The law firm of MacGregor, Spurling, Hart and Trakimas Esquires occupies this classical revival house at 105 Kenoza Avenue.

REGAN FORD, INC.

In 1944, as World War II was drawing to a close, Frank Regan, Sr., opened a Ford dealership in Haverhill with his cousin, Joseph S. Regan. The business was incorporated as Regan Motor Company, Inc., in January 1946. The firm occupied a five-story building overlooking the Merrimack River at 65 Water Street.

The immediate postwar years were a struggle, but the Regans' love for the business, community, and family kept their dreams focused on a soon-to-be flourishing venture. The intersection of Main and Water streets, better known as White's Corner, was an extremely busy section of Haverhill.

In 1951 Joseph Regan died, leaving his interest in the business to his wife, Anastasia Lafey Regan. Frank Sr., however, continued to assure their future by running the firm alone.

Frank Regan, Sr., was born in Haverhill and attended St. James High School and Boston College from which he was graduated in 1927. Soon after college he worked in New York and Connecticut, but returned to his native city where he married the former C. Louise Dwyer.

Frank Regan, Sr., co-founder of Regan Motor Company, Inc.

Throughout his lifetime he was closely associated with the alumni association of Boston College.

Frank Sr. believed that the success of the city was to a large part dictated by the strengths of local businesses, both large and small. He believed there was a great potential for growth and, therefore, readily accepted the suggestion to become an investor in and founder of the Greater Haverhill Foundation. This group of business leaders developed the Ward Hill Industrial Park. Their efforts set the pace for the redevelopment and expansion of Haverhill that has reached its pinnacle in the 1980s.

Regan Motor Company, Inc., remained on Water Street until 1967, when urban renewal forced the firm to consider relocation. Frank Regan, Sr., viewed this as an appropriate turning point in the life of the business to signal his retirement. He decided to leave the decision of a new site for the dealership to his son, Frank Jr., who would guide the business into the future.

Frank Regan, Jr., was born in Haverhill and graduated from St. James High School in 1950. He graduated from Merrimack College in North Andover in 1954 with a degree in Economics. A two-year tour in the U.S. Army ended in 1956. Soon after, he began his career in the automobile business with his father, and in October of that year he married the former Mary D. Cronin, also of Haverhill. For the next 10 years he was involved in all details of the Water Street firm, which gave him a solid background for his future as a dealer.

In 1967, when Frank Jr. became president, he was joined by W. Sidney Lafey as treasurer. In June 1969 the firm's name was changed to Regan-Lafey Ford.

By that time the company was in its new quarters at 501 Broadway. The location reflected Frank's belief that the growth potential of Haverhill would shift from the inner city to the area along Interstate 495. Ten years after moving to its new location, Lafey retired and Frank Regan, Jr., became the sole owner. The name of the company was then changed to its present title of Regan Ford, Inc.

Frank Regan, Jr., had a great love for Haverhill. He was a member

Frank Regan, Jr., president.

of the Greater Haverhill Chamber of Commerce and a past member of service and civic groups. He was a member of the local automobile dealers' group as well as a member of the New England Ford Dealers' Association and the Massachusetts Dealers' Automobile Association. He also had a long-term association with the Men of Merrimack College. However, the real centers of his life were his family—his parents, and only brother, Dr. J. Joseph Regan—and his business. He was fortunate to love what he did for a living; he truly enjoyed doing business with people from all walks of life.

Regan Ford's customer and employee loyalty can only be attributed to Frank's sincere respect for others and the drive that he had for hard

The predecessor to the current Ford dealership, Regan Motor Company, Inc., was located at 65 Water Street, Haverhill, when this photograph was taken in 1936.

work. There are hundreds of Fords in the Haverhill area that bear a front license plate that says "We ♥ Regan Ford." It was Frank's idea to have such a plate, but even he was surprised with its acceptance by customers.

As the business grew, the Broadway location was expanded to include a larger service department and, in 1986, an entirely new body shop. Throughout the past 10 years he worked closely with Ford Motor Company to create a larger and more efficient dealership for the greater Haverhill area.

On May 10, 1987, Frank Regan, Jr., died of a heart attack. His family has made the commitment to continue the tradition of providing a quality dealership backed by service and friendly personal attention. The third generation of Regans, along with Mary D. Regan, are working to make this possible. The business their grandfather founded 43 years ago has changed greatly, but the basic beliefs are well remembered.

Ann Regan has assumed the greater part of her father's responsibilities but believes that teamwork by family and employees will continue to keep Regan Ford strong. Timothy Regan heads the Leasing and Rental divisions, which he began developing five years ago. Kevin Regan knows that quality service work has led to the success and reputation of the dealership, and his knowledge and assistance in the service area will assure the commitment to customers' needs. The other Regan children, Dr. Michael F. Regan and Elizabeth, have joined the other family members as directors on the Regan Ford, Inc., board.

The new generation of Regans is dedicated to continuing the tradition of quality and service established by Frank Sr. and brought to maturity by Frank Jr. This should assure that for many more years hundreds of Fords in the area will declare to oncoming traffic, "We ♥ Regan Ford."

A tradition of quality and service established through the years is carried on by a new generation at Regan Ford, Inc., 501 Broadway, Haverhill. Photo taken in 1987.

DYETEX, INC.

In 1939 Joseph Shain of Boston joined Raymond Cowan of Haverhill in a business venture. They had met at Lowell Technological Institute, and both graduated with degrees in dye chemistry.

Cowan and Shain decided to locate the business in Haverhill to take advantage of the city's good, available work force and low-cost factory space. Their first location was on Walnut Street; later they moved the business to River Street; and in 1953 they bought the mills along Little River on Stevens and Winter streets.

The business was initially known as Cowan & Shain, Inc., dyers and treaters of narrow fabrics, that is, webbing, elastic, ribbon, belting, etc. Later Pentucket Textiles was added as a division. Much of their output was utilized by the shoe industry, so the Haverhill location was ideal.

In 1960 Raymond Cowan died, and shortly thereafter Joseph Shain created DYETEX, Inc., a division to skein dye yarn for the hand-knitting and apparel trade. In 1966 Steven Shain joined his father in the business and helped move the company from the narrow fabric field into dyeing yarn for the ladies' knit dress industry.

Continuing to operate as Cowan and Shain, Inc. (later named Little River Dyers, Inc.), and DYETEX, Inc., the company employed 75 people during its peak period. Currently the firm employs 40 people and is primarily a dyer of novelty yarns, including mohair, cashmere, and angora. The company can produce a rainbow of custom colors to fit the need of any customer in batches of 25 to 400 pounds. Yarns dyed by DYETEX grace women all over the world.

DYETEX occupies the most historic industrial site in Haverhill, one that has been occupied by mills since the seventeenth century. In 1804 Ezekiel Hale, Sr., the patriarch of the prominent Hale family, built the dam on Little River and established a cotton mill on the site, producing red flannel.

Hale's son, Ezekiel Hale, Jr., bought his father's business in 1833, and E.J.M. Hale joined the family firm two years later. E.J.M. Hale, Haverhill's best-known philanthropist, gave his name to Hale Hospital and helped found the Haverhill Public Library. In 1835 the mill was partially destroyed by fire, and a new brick factory was built. It became the largest producer of red flannel in the world. In 1839 Ezekiel Jr. left the management of the business to his son.

When Ezekiel Jr. demanded the return of the business and his son refused, there ensued one of the area's

Joseph Shain (seated), treasurer, with son Steven, president, of DYETEX, Inc.

most scandalous law suits, *Hale* v. *Hale,* that finally ended with the mills back in the hands of the father. In 1855 he sold the mills to Captain Nathaniel Stevens at an auction. The Stevens family had owned the mills for nearly a century when they were subdivided, and Cowan and Shain bought the portion nearest Winter Street.

A native of Boston, Joseph Shain joined his partner, Haverhill native Cowan, in supporting Haverhill. They were both active in the chamber of commerce and in the Greater Haverhill Foundation, which developed the Ward Hill Industrial Park. They participated in United Fund campaigns and took an active interest in the affairs of the city, particularly those things that improved the business climate and the quality of life.

Steven Shain and his wife, Carol, are Haverhill residents. They continue the tradition of working to make the city a good place to live for their children, Jonathan, Ross, and Dara, and for all its citizens.

Joseph and Steven Shain of DYETEX, Inc., carry on a centuries-old tradition of manufacturing along the banks of the Little River at Hale's Dam.

DYETEX, Inc., occupies this historic site at Hale's Dam on the Little River in Haverhill. A mill has been located there since the seventeenth century.

DOLE & CHILDS FUNERAL HOME

In 1839 two brothers-in-law, John P. Randall and Joseph H. Cummings, opened a furniture business on Merrimack Street that made and sold burial coffins. Above the store they established J.H. Cummings, Furnishing Undertakers. In 1882 the business was relocated to a storefront at 39 Main Street.

The firm was sold in 1886 to a well-known stable owner, Fred G. Richards, who later became mayor of Haverhill, and a prominent banker, George H. Dole. They changed the name to Richards and Dole. Richards' stable was the oldest stand in Haverhill. There one could rent Tally-Ho coaches, barges, hacks, carriages, and find accommodations for more than 100 horses. This partnership gave the business extensive livery equipment as well as adding new funeral equipment.

Richards died in 1895, and George H. Childs, who had been an employee for four years, bought into the business. Since that time the firm has been known as Dole & Childs Funeral Home.

By 1919 the company had become fully motorized. A modern garage replaced the livery stable at 34 Stage Street, and a space that had housed 36 horses could now accommodate 50 cars. Dole & Childs was one of the best equipped establishments in the state.

Earle W. Graffam became an active partner in the firm upon his return from World War I. Childs died in 1921, and Dole passed away two years later. A corporation was formed in 1923, and George L. Riley joined Graffam in the business the following year.

After nearly a century of service to greater Haverhill, Graffam recognized that a more modern approach to the funeral business was needed. In the past storefront funeral parlors had served the public well since wakes and funeral services were gen-

J.H. Cummings, Furnishing Undertaker, at 39 Main Street when this photograph was taken, was the predecessor of today's Dole & Childs Funeral Home.

erally held in the home. Now, with more people living in apartments and smaller quarters, the new concept of the funeral home, where all services could be combined under

This beautiful example of Victorian Stick-style architecture, considered to be one of the most perfect in New England, is the Dole & Childs Funeral Home. Built in 1879 by the heirs of Rufus Chase, it held the first funeral in a funeral home in Haverhill on March 15, 1933.

one roof, was gaining in popularity.

In 1932 Dole & Childs acquired the property at 148 Main Street from the Knights of Columbus. This beautiful home, considered one of the most perfect examples of Victorian Stick-style architecture in New England, was built by the heirs of Rufus Chase in 1879. The woodwork and the staircase were carved by Italian artisans imported for the project. The first funeral in a funeral home in Haverhill was held in this magnificent home on March 15, 1933.

Graffam died in 1959 and Riley retired nine years later. The business was now headed by Wesley J. Shaw, who joined the firm before World War II, and H. Lee Powell, who entered the business after the war. Eric V. Pare joined the operation in 1982.

Although personnel has changed over the years, the business has maintained the name of Dole & Childs. The oldest funeral home in Haverhill, it carries on a long and rich tradition, and continues to serve the people of greater Haverhill with compassion, caring, and honesty.

HAMEL CHARITABLE FOUNDATION, INC.

On October 15, 1947, Louis H. Hamel established Hamel Charitable Foundation, Inc., devoted exclusively to promoting religious, charitable, scientific, literary, and educational purposes within the United States.

The Hamel Foundation, established and guided by Hamel until his death in 1975, is currently overseen by his wife, Dorothy Berry Hamel. "Mr. Hamel made his money with the help of a lot of good people—good workers—here in Haverhill. He left this legacy to the people of the city who helped him succeed," explains Donald Beaton, who is office manager of the foundation.

Hamel made a considerable amount of money in the leather business in Haverhill. A self-made man of great abilities but limited formal education, he continued to learn all his life and was a strong supporter of education in the Merrimack Valley. He was a loyal supporter of his church and, as the father of seven children, deeply concerned about the welfare of all young people in the community.

Thus, education and young people are the two major themes of the foundation's activities. A third is projects broadly benefiting the City of Haverhill and the region.

Many educational institutions and programs have received Hamel support. Most notable is Merrimack College. Hamel was one of a small group of valley businessmen who planned and developed the college, founded in neighboring North Andover by the Order of St. Augustine. The Hamels presented the college with the statue of Christ the Teacher, which graces the entrance of the campus. Large contributions were also made to the library and to the infirmary, which is named for Mr. Hamel.

Bradford College has also benefited from the generosity of the foundation as have the Haverhill Trade School, forerunner of Whittier Vocational and Technical School, and Haverhill High School. Two buildings that housed the trade school were donated to the city by the foundation to enable the school to meet the increasing demands for vocational education. The foundation has long supported the Dollars for Scholars program at Haverhill High as well as a Hamel Leather Award in Chemistry. Through the Kiwanis Club the foundation has helped recognize local honor society students. The New England College Fund has received support, and traineeships have been funded at the Museum of Science.

Children and young people have always been a major interest of the foundation. Support goes to many summer camps, the Boy Scouts of America, the Girl's Club, the Haverhill Day Care Center, Police Athletic League, the YMCA, and many more. The Haverhill Boy's Club building fund received support as did the Pediatric Department of the old Hale Hospital and the new Hale Hospital building fund. The Public Library building fund also benefited.

In the realm of support for the city, in addition to the hospital and library, the foundation has supported arts programs, the police communications system, Merrivista Community Center, and Winnikinni Foundation.

Louis Hamel was proud of Haverhill. When the foundation learned that there was no painting in Washington to honor William Moody, the only Haverhill native to serve on the U.S. Supreme Court, and that he was the only justice without a portrait, the foundation donated funds for the painting. The foundation supported Haverhill's bid to be an All-American City and can always be relied upon to support worthy causes that improve the area.

Louis H. Hamel's legacy continues to benefit the city each year as the foundation supports programs for education, youth, and, increasingly, the elderly. Where there are needs, there one will find his Hamel Charitable Foundation, guided by Dorothy Hamel, lending support and working to make Haverhill and environs a better place for all.

DESIGN PARTNERSHIP ARCHITECTS, INC.

In 1977 Angelo Petrozzelli and his wife, Kathy, had just returned to the Boston area from Woodstock, Vermont. They were looking for a home and heard that Haverhill had wonderful houses at reasonable prices. They came to look, liked what they saw, and bought a home in the Walnut Square neighborhood.

Petrozzelli was in architectural practice with a firm in North Reading. Originally from Boston, he was educated at Northeastern University and the Boston Architectural Center, and in 1972 received a master's degree in architecture from M.I.T.

By the late 1970s he was ready to be a principal in his own firm and in 1979 formed Design Partnership Architects, Inc., with Brian Libby, another architect. Petrozzelli and Libby opened their office on the second floor of the Coombs Building on Washington Square and immediately became involved in the revitalization of the Washington Street historic district. Their first project was the Merrimack Valley Regional Transit Authority Station on Washington Square. While working on the station they got to know their landlord, Adam Rizzo, who shared their vision of what the area could become. In addition to the Coombs Building, Rizzo also owned the Whittier Hotel, and the firm began to do work for him on both structures.

. Petrozzelli also became active in his neighborhood, heading the Walnut Square Neighborhood Association and later the citywide Neighborhood Coalition. He served on the Haverhill Growth Alliance board and the board of the Haverhill Foundation for Improved Housing, a non-profit group working to rehabilitate the city's historic inner-city housing.

Work with housing rehabilitation led the firm into two pilot projects with Family Mutual Savings Bank, one on Vine Street and one on Middlesex Street in Bradford. These two projects set the standard for quality in housing rehabilitation during the years that followed. The firm also did the design work for a condominium created by the Housing Foundation on Arlington Street called Davis Lane.

While work in the neighborhood progressed, Petrozzelli was using the signage program of the City of Haverhill to create sign-bearing awnings that made a strong visual impact in the slowly reviving downtown historic district. He also became involved in major rehabilitation projects: the Currier-Sanders Block, Pedro Diegos' restaurant, the Finney Block, and the Tilton Block. In fact, Petrozzelli has been involved in more than 25 projects in the Washington Street district. As Mayor William H. Ryan recently put it, "Much of the responsibility for this comeback (by the district) can be credited to the improvisational and creative work of Design Partnership Architects, led by its principal architect, Angelo Petrozzelli."

Design Partnership Architects, Inc., has been involved in many of the rehabilitation projects in Haverhill's inner city, including the Tilton Block (right) and the Whittier Hotel (below). The firm's sign-bearing awning creations make a strong visual impact in the downtown historic district.

Petrozzelli has also done new construction, notably the Haverhill Alliance Church; Promises to Keep, a restaurant in Derry, New Hampshire; the Magic Pan on Newbury Street and Cafe Amalfi, both in Boston; Dennent's Wharf in Castine, Maine; and an addition to the Queechee Inn at Marshland Farm in Queechee, Vermont. Petrozzelli has also done historic preservation work outside Haverhill in areas including Lynn, Salem, Roxbury, and Fitchburg. He is currently supervising projects from Maine to Barbados.

POWELL SUPPLY COMPANY

Powell Supply Company, a wholesale electrical distributor, began in 1921 when John D. Osgood opened an electrical contracting firm on Essex Street. The business was continued after his death in 1934 by his son, Harold Osgood, who moved the operation to Pleasant Street and began to sell electrical supplies wholesale.

In 1954 the firm was purchased by John Colter and Leota C. Bailey, who had been a bookkeeper for the firm for many years. After Colter's death only four years later, Bailey became the sole owner. In 1968 Bailey sold the firm to Nelson M. Powell III, who moved the company to its present location when urban renewal forced it out of downtown Haverhill.

In 1983 William A. Fallon acquired the business. Fallon, a graduate of Boston College, had spent much of his professional life as an executive with the U.S. subsidiary of a British firm. When he decided to buy his own company he made a national search that led him to Haverhill and Powell Supply. "The business was what I was looking for, and returning to the greater Boston area was a plus for my wife and me" says Fallon.

Powell Supply Company has a commanding location at 15 Thornton Avenue overlooking the Merrimack River and the intersection of Interstate 495 and routes 110 and 113. Not only is the firm visible from the highways and Westgate Shopping Center, it is easily accessible to its wide range of customers. Powell Supply Company has a large showroom where a home owner or condominium developer can select all the fixtures for a single-family home or a 400-unit complex. There is also a separate entrance for the wholesale counter area where electrical contractors can purchase any material needed for jobs ranging from a simple repair to all the original material for a multistoried commercial, industrial, or residential complex.

An increasing percentage of Powell Supply Company's business is with large corporations such as Digital, Wang, and Apollo, and with governmental facilities such as the Portsmouth Naval Yard. Currently the firm has three full-time outside salespeople in addition to the counter and showroom staffs. Powell services schools, hospitals, military installations, and even power stations; Seabrook Nuclear Power Station is a customer.

Bill Fallon heads a firm that has grown from what was the smallest independent electrical wholesaler in the Merrimack Valley in 1968 to become the largest in 1987. His staff of 28 employees can deal with any customer need. The versatile, well-balanced staff includes such veterans as Mary Ritchie of Bradford, who has been with the company for 45 years, and John Burke, vice-president of operations, who has more than 30 years of service.

Fallon sees the firm's role as continuing to serve its traditional constituencies—electrical contractors, industrial, municipal, and retail.

William A. Fallon (left), president and owner of Powell Supply Company, with showroom director Mary Ritchie, who has been with the firm for 45 years, and John Burke, vice-president of operations, with more than 30 years of service.

The company's industrial accounts are obviously a major growth area as the Merrimack Valley booms. But Fallon also plans to expand service to the individual customer by expanding the counter area to service the needs of do-it-yourself home owners.

The Powell Supply Product Digest, a long list of product types with brand names available from the firm, gives vivid evidence of the remarkable range of merchandise available. Whether one wants a chandelier for a dining room, an alarm system for a school, a generator for a factory, a bug killer for a summer place, or a truckload of conduit, the company can supply it.

For longer than a half-century the firm, under many names, has served the needs of the Merrimack Valley. Bill Fallon sees a future for Powell Supply Company that involves building upon that fine history.

EAGLE-TRIBUNE

When the *Eagle-Tribune* acceded to repeated requests from readers and advertisers to have a greater presence in Haverhill, it decided to treat Haverhill the same way it treats Lawrence—as a community it cares about.

The *Eagle-Tribune* is one of a dying breed of newspapers, home-owned and home-managed. "When I walk down the street, people greet me by name," says publisher Irving E. Rogers, Jr., the fourth generation of the Rogers family to guide Essex County's largest newspaper. "I'm accountable to those people for the quality of newspaper we produce and for the sense of community interest we exhibit."

So the *Eagle-Tribune* expanded its Haverhill coverage by creating a special edition for Haverhill and its suburbs, by opening an office downtown in the heart of the historic Washington Square area, and by hiring Haverhill residents to staff that office, headed by Bernard "Barney" Gallagher, whose service to newspapering in Haverhill spanned 50 years.

"We didn't hire Barney because he had been around for a long time," says Rogers. "We hired him because he was the best newsman in Haverhill, because he knew Haverhill better than anyone in town, and because he loved Haverhill."

Gallagher and the rest of the paper's news, advertising, and circulation staff set about to create the only newspaper serving Haverhill that is:

home-owned and home-managed with a history of intense involvement in Merrimack Valley communities that goes back nearly 120 years; also covering the rest of the lower Merrimack Valley, including those Haverhill suburbs in both Massachusetts and New Hampshire; supporting full-time Boston and Concord, New Hampshire, statehouse, and Washington bureaus to bring local residents news of what their state legislators and congressmen are doing; rich in sports coverage, including hometown staffing of New England professional teams and lively, complete local sports reports; providing lively photo coverage in both color and black and white; published seven days a week so that readers always have news when it is fresh; and a member of the New England News Exchange, a direct tie with the Boston radio and TV market, so that Haverhill's many accomplishments do not go unnoticed in greater Boston.

It is just this sort of vitality that the *Eagle-Tribune* is famous for. It was started in 1867 in the form of the *Essex Eagle,* one of the forerunners of today's *Eagle-Tribune.* The other forerunner, the *Evening Tribune,* was organized in 1890.

In 1898 Alexander Rogers used funds loaned to him by his father to

The Eagle-Tribune *Haverhill office is located at 52 Washington Street in the city's downtown National Register historic district.*

purchase both newspapers in partnership with Henry F. Hildreth. This partnership published both papers for a decade until Hildreth's death, when Rogers bought Hildreth's interest from his heirs.

In 1968, a century after the *Daily Eagle's* founding, the two papers were merged as the newly formed *Eagle-Tribune* moved into a state-of-the-art newspaper publishing plant on Route 114 in North Andover. Included were huge color presses that have since been expanded to give the newspaper even more printing and color capacity. A decade later the *Eagle-Tribune* started its Sunday Edition, an edition that enjoyed immediate success.

Also located in the Route 114 plant is Eagle-Tribune Printing, a commercial printing company that handles everything from wedding invitations to books.

In 1968 the Eagle-Tribune *moved into this state-of-the-art plant on Route 114 in North Andover.*

DeMOULAS & MARKET BASKET

Arthur DeMoulas, an immigrant who founded DeMoulas & Market Basket 70 years ago, ran a typical neighborhood grocery store in Lowell, Massachusetts, to serve the needs of his community. DeMoulas & Market Basket, as we know it today, evolved from a corner store where customers ran a tab, ordered groceries by phone, and had them delivered to their homes.

When the three major cities in the Merrimack Valley—Haverhill, Lowell, and Lawrence—were joined

The first DeMoulas Market on Dummer Street in Lowell. Photo circa 1939

by Interstate 495, accessibility and an insurgence of development was the result. In 1966 DeMoulas & Market Basket opened its first store in Haverhill at Westgate Plaza, and six years later cut the ribbon at a second location in the heart of Haverhill's downtown. Today there are four facilities operating in the greater Haverhill area, and the tiny superette of 1917 has grown to 41 supermarkets in 30 communities.

For more than 20 years De-Moulas & Market Basket has been an integral part of Haverhill, providing thousands of jobs through its shopping centers and supermar-

The first DeMoulas & Market Basket store to open in Haverhill in 1966.

kets. It shows its appreciation for community support by dedicating time and resources to philanthropic institutions. These organizations include hospitals; schools and universities; churches, temples, and religious groups; and other local charities. DeMoulas & Market Basket is a family-oriented, people-minded, community-involved food store.

The growth of DeMoulas & Market Basket began in 1950, when national supermarket chains already

dominated the area. In order to compete, DeMoulas & Market Basket enlarged its variety store to a superette. The store was successful, but chances for an independent grocer surviving outside of its own neighborhood were slim. In 1957, despite the high risk and discouraging words from area businessmen, a second DeMoulas Market opened in Lowell. Since then DeMoulas & Market Basket has opened stores annually in Massachusetts and New Hampshire.

In 1963 DeMoulas & Market Basket implemented its Profit Sharing Plan, which, as it implies, enables employees to share in the profits of their company. DeMoulas & Market Basket believes a prospering company has an obligation to its people and that to only pay a person a decent wage for many years of service is inadequate. The plan is 100 percent contributory, made possible by the hard work of everyone associated with DeMoulas & Market Basket. Within the food industry, this is one reason the Profit Sharing Plan is second to none.

Today the company is prospering by adhering to traditional but not outdated values. Now in its third generation, DeMoulas & Market Basket will continue to grow as long as it maintains its original commitment to its customers, its associates, and their families.

The downtown Haverhill DeMoulas & Market Basket store opened in 1972.

ESSEX COUNTY GAS COMPANY

On February 23, 1853, a group of local businessmen founded the Haverhill Gas Light Company. During the spring and summer of that year a group of brick buildings were erected on Winter Street where illuminating gas for lighting purposes was produced. The original plant consisted of a coal gas house, boiler room, office, stable, and a small, 6,000-cubic-foot gas storage tank.

The use of gas was limited to street and home lighting until 1894, when gas stoves for cooking came on the market. As electricity replaced gas as a source of lighting, the company turned to supplying fuel for not only cooking but also water heating. The firm also expanded into adjacent towns, selling gas to the Amesbury and Salisbury Gas Company, the Gas Department of the Haverhill Electric Company in Newburyport, and the Northshore Gas Company in the Ipswich area. The Haverhill company bought all three firms between 1923 and 1950.

Haverhill Gas Company continued to manufacture gas until natural gas was introduced in November 1951. At that time the firm converted all its customers' appliances to natural gas operation.

In the late 1960s the company recognized a potential energy production shortage before the OPEC oil embargo brought the energy production crisis into the spotlight in 1973. Fortunately for customers the management's early recognition of the energy shortage allowed time to prepare and build a liquefied natural gas storage facility that was placed in operation in September 1972. It can produce 24 million cubic feet of supplemental gas per day and has a storage capacity equivalent to 400 million cubic feet of gas. In addition to supplying peak-saving requirements, the facility also provides a source of standby gas to further guarantee continuity of service to customers if the pipeline supply is interrupted or curtailed.

The gas used in area homes and businesses is natural gas routinely purchased from the Tennessee Gas Pipeline Company under a contract on file with the Massachusetts Department of Public Utilities and the Federal Energy Regulatory Commission. The gas is taken into the interconnected distribution system at three separate locations: Haverhill at the north end and Wenham and Essex at the south end.

In 1973 the firm was notified by the Haverhill Housing Authority that its headquarters on Merrimack Street would be taken by urban renewal. A search for a new corporate headquarters began. Located on Hunt Road in Amesbury, with easy access from Interstate 495 and close proximity to Interstate 95, the new corporate headquarters and operations service center is easily accessible to all customers. Now serving 32,200 customers in 17 cities and towns, the utility has been known as Essex County Gas Company since 1983. Ninety percent of its customers are residential, with the balance consisting of all types of commercial and industrial users.

For 134 years Essex County Gas Company has been providing safe, reliable service for its growing number of customers. As Charles E. Billups, president and chairman of the board, puts it, "Our employees' commitment statement continues to provide the philosophy and action programs to serve our current customers and to attract new ones."

With a proud tradition behind it, Essex County Gas Company looks to a future of continuing service and progress.

ESSEX COUNTY GAS COMPANY EMPLOYEE COMMITMENT STATEMENT

Because customers are the focus of our business and provide our jobs, we, the team at Essex County Gas Company, are committed to helping our customers use our product safely, economically, and efficiently.

Our aim is to meet the needs of our customers and community through quick response, cooperation, effective communications, and by striving for excellence in everything we do.

We are people serving people.

SPRING HILL FARM DAIRY

Spring Hill Farm Dairy was started in 1902, when Randolph K. Rogers purchased a house and 12.5 acres of land in the Ward Hill section of Haverhill. Randolph, recovering from a train accident, hoped to become self-sufficient with a few cows, some poultry, and a small vegetable plot.

In 1927, after his son Harold graduated from Essex County Agricultural School, they increased the dairy herd and began raising vegetables and small fruits for the local market. As the business grew, Harold purchased every available acre of land adjoining the farm until it grew to 198 acres of rich river bottom land.

For nearly 20 years the farm business stayed diversified with some poultry, a small dairy herd, vegetable gardens, and small orchards. However, with shortages of labor, farm machinery, and supplies as a result of World War II, it became necessary to concentrate on just one aspect of the farm business. Harold decided to increase the dairy herd and sell the milk retail in the greater Haverhill area.

In the late 1950s and early 1960s, when Harold's two sons finished school, he supported their efforts in agronomy. Thus, Richard, who was interested in raising crops, herd management, and machinery, assumed management of these segments of the farm. Dale, who enjoyed selling and working with the finished product, took over the management of the processing plant and milk routes, and in 1980 opened a small retail outlet at the plant.

In the early 1980s another farm product emerged as a potential profit maker: Spring water became a marketable item. The Rogerses took a look at the springs that gave

The Rogers family and horse in front of the old homestead as Randolph K. Rogers began his farming career in 1902.

the farm its name. Now clear, pure water is pumped through stainless-steel pipes to the bottling plant. Spring Hill is one of only two firms in New England where water is actually bottled "at the source." Spring Hill Farm water is sold not only in the Boston area but to 25 large distributors who sell it throughout New England.

Using all available resources, as woodland was cleared a small firewood business developed. With the popularity of "Pick Your Own," a small acreage for strawberries and early peas was planted.

Stephen Rogers, son of Richard, is the first of the fourth generation of Rogers to become involved with the family business. Stephen is particularly interested in herd health, selective breeding of the large herd of holstein cattle, and crop rotation and the management of feed for the animals.

Harold and Dale, sons of Dale Rogers, although still in school, are working with their father with processing and distribution of milk and water.

Spring Hill Farm Dairy has the distinction of being the last surviving milk business in Haverhill that produces, processes, and delivers its own milk.

From a humble beginning of one horse, two cows, no telephone, no electricity, no running water, and no paved road, Spring Hill Farm Dairy can now boast of a top producing dairy herd, a fleet of trucks and tractors, modern farm machinery, and a view of green fields sloping down to the Merrimack River for almost a mile. While to the north and east Spring Hill Farm Dairy is penned in by the Ward Hill Industrial Parks and to the south with a growing community of new homes, its owners tenaciously hold on to its green oasis amidst all this and pray they can continue to wake up to the song of birds and the scent of new-mown hay for yet a fifth generation.

Harold Rogers, Sr. (left), with son Richard (right), grandson Harold (center), and some of their modern trucks and tractors.

HOWARD JOHNSON MOTOR LODGE

In 1965 Richard E. Blinn of Groveland and his partner, Bostonian Hervey Solar, built a motor lodge in Haverhill that has become "a home away from home" for many visitors. Each year 45,000 guests stay at the motel, a Howard Johnson franchise.

The lodge is located just off Interstate 495 at 401 Lowell Avenue. Adjacent to the facility, but not owned by Blinn and Solar, is a familiar orange, blue, and white Howard Johnson's restaurant, a handy source of meals for lodge guests.

Opening with 61 rooms in 1965, the Howard Johnson Motor Lodge has grown with Haverhill. In the winter of 1973, at the height of a recession, Blinn added 28 more units. In October 1986 another 40 guest rooms were completed, making a grand total of 129 units. A function room to hold 100 people was also added at that time to expand the function capacity of the lodge, which also has two other smaller rooms—the Century Room and Powwow Room.

For the past 15 years the establishment has been managed by Ronald Young of Salisbury. Young attributes the Howard Johnson Motor Lodge's success to hard work and the personal touch. The aim of the staff and management is to provide guests with "own home convenience." This involves, according to Young, "cleanliness. This is what everyone looks for first in a place in which they are going to stay, and they must be treated as human beings. If not, then they just won't come back. We specialize in both these things, and it has worked out well."

Blinn points out that tourists are more or less seasonal in their use of the lodge, but the backbone of his business is "our commercial accounts." Blinn says you would have to characterize the tourist business as the frosting on the facility's cake, but there would not be much cake without the businessmen who use the lodge continually throughout the year. "We service greater Haverhill; we are the only motel in town, and also draw many business people from Lawrence-area firms. It's really the name of the game," he says.

Approximately 60 percent of the guests are repeat visitors. They are greeted by Young's familiar face and by a reception desk staff that average 8 to 10 years of service. "This means," says Young, "that we not only greet a guest by name, but we often know him well enough to ask after the health of a family member who was sick when he last stayed with us."

The motor lodge also has a long-standing relationship with several trucking firms. Plug-in units are even provided for the big diesels. Howard Johnson Motor Lodge in Haverhill has been a routine overnight stop for some firms for 20 years.

Whether tourist or business traveler, all guests will find a spotlessly clean, well-run facility. The hostelry won an award for these qualities in 1977, the first in New England to do so. Add the personal touch of a staff that really cares about the comfort of its guests and will remember them if they return, and that is the secret of success that has allowed the Haverhill Howard Johnson Motor Lodge to flourish along with its community and the surrounding area.

The Howard Johnson Motor Lodge at 401 Lowell Avenue is a home away from home for thousands of travelers each year.

PATRONS

The following individuals, companies, and organizations have made a valuable commitment to the quality of this publication. Windsor Publications, Bradford College, and the Greater Haverhill Chamber of Commerce gratefully acknowledge their participation in *A New England City: Haverhill, Massachusetts.*

A Brand New Touch
Anthony-Brooks Insurance Agency, Incorporated*
Bethany Homes, Inc.
Chesley T. Bixby
Cedardale, Incorporated*
Sandra Libbey Charron
Compugraphic Corporation*
Hartley and Joan Cranton
DeMoulas & Market Basket*
Design Partnership Architects, Inc.*
Dole & Childs Funeral Home*
Mr. and Mrs. Chester J. Domoracki
Dyetex, Inc.*
Eagle-Tribune*
Essex County Gas Company*
E-Z Way Cleaners
Falcone Piano Company*
The Family Mutual Savings Bank*
Hamel Charitable Foundation, Inc.*
The Haverhill Co-operative Bank*
Haverhill High School Social Studies Department
Haverhill Paperboard*
Howard Johnson Motor Lodge*
Kenoza Vending Co., Inc.*
The T. Philip Kosmes Family
C. Frank Linnehan & Son Funeral Service*
MacGregor, Spurling, Hart and Trakimas Esquires*
Frederick E. Malcolm Insurance Agency, Inc.*
Barbara J. Minchey
Marilyn D. Moore
Nagle & MacMillan
Nefor Engineering and Manufacturing Company, Inc.
Nofsker Component Products, Inc.*
William J. Nofsker
North East Cultural Arts Center, Inc.
Northern Essex Community College*
Ogden Martin Systems, Inc.*
Pentucket Bank
Phillips, Gerstein, Holber, LaFlamme, Migliori & Barron*
Plaistow Cooperative Bank
Pope Machinery, Inc.*
Powell Supply Company*

Regan Ford, Inc.*
Rotary Club of Haverhill, Massachusetts
Sheehan and Schiavoni*
Soroptimist International Haverhill/ Merrimack Valley Chapter
Spring Hill Farm Dairy*
Tyler Construction Co., Inc.
Youngblood Plumbing and Heating Company, Inc.
Youngblood Mechanical Contractors, Inc.*

*Partners in Progress of *A New England City: Haverhill, Massachusetts.* The histories of these companies and organizations appear in Chapter 7, beginning on page 87.

BIBLIOGRAPHY

Books and collections

"An Historical Sketch of Haverhill, in the County of Essex, and Commonwealth of Massachusetts: with Bibliographical Notices." In *Massachusetts Historical Society Proceedings.* 2d series (1815). Vol. 4, 121-174.

Arrington, Benjamin F., ed. *Municipal History of Essex County in Massachusetts.* Tercentary ed. 4 vols. New York: Lewis Historical Publishing, 1922.

Bedford, Henry F. *Socialism and the Workers in Massachusetts, 1886-1912.* Amherst: University of Massachusetts Press, 1966.

Bedford, Henry F. "The Haverhill Social Democrat: Spokesman for Socialism." *Labor History* 2, no. 1 (Winter 1961): 83-89.

Bedford, Henry F. "The Socialist Movement in Haverhill." *Essex Institute Historical Collections* XCIX, no. 1 (January 1963): 33-47.

Blewett, Mary H. "The Union of Sex and Craft in the Haverhill Shoe Strike of 1895." *Labor History* 20, no. 3 (Summer 1979): 352-375.

Chase, George Wingate. *The History of Haverhill, Massachusetts.* 1861. Reprint. Haverhill: Haverhill Historical Society, 1983.

Cole, Arthur H. "Boyhood in the Golden Age." *Essex Institute Historical Collections* CII, no. 2 (April 1967): 89-139.

Conditions in the Shoe Industry in Haverhill, Mass., 1928. Bulletin no. 483. Washington, D.C.: GPO, 1929.

Davis, Horace B. *Shoes: The Workers and the Industry.* New York: International Publishers, 1940.

Editorial staff of the War Records Committee. *Haverhill in World War II.* The City of Haverhill, 1946.

Fuess, Claude M., ed. *The Story of Essex County.* 4 vols. New York: American Historical Society, 1935.

Haverhill Board of Trade. *History of the City of Haverhill, Massachusetts . . .* Haverhill: Haverhill Board of Trade, 1905.

Hazard, Blanche E. *The Organization of the Boot and Shoe Industry in Massachusetts Before 1875.* Cambridge: Harvard University Press, 1921.

Hudon, Paul. *The Valley and Its People: An Illustrated History of the Lower Merrimack.* Woodland Hills: Windsor Publications, 1982.

Hurd, D. Hamilton, ed. *History of Essex County, Massachusetts.* 2 vols. Philadelphia: J.W. Lewis, 1888.

Labor Conditions in the Shoe Industry in Massachusetts, 1920-1924. Bulletin no. 384. Washington, D.C.: GPO, 1925.

Moody, Robert, ed. *The Saltonstall Papers, 1607-1815.* 2 vols. Boston: Massachusetts Historical Society, 1972.

Norton, Thomas L. *Trade Union Policies in the Massachusetts Shoe Industry, 1919-1929.* New York: Columbia University, 1932.

O'Malley, Patricia Trainor. *Sacred Hearts Parish, Bradford, Massachusetts: A 75th Anniversary History.* Bradford: 1985.

Standard History of Essex County, Massachusetts. Boston: C.J. Jewett, 1878.

Unpublished manuscripts

Merrill, Isaac W. Diary. 7 vols. Haverhill Public Library Special Collections.

Miller, Grant. "The Shoe Industry of Haverhill, Massachusetts, from 1905 to 1930." Master's thesis, University of New Hampshire, 1974.

O'Malley, Patricia Trainor. "The Annexation Issue in Haverhill and Bradford, 1865-1896." 1968.

O'Malley, Patricia Trainor. "Rowley, Massachusetts: 1640-1730—Dissent, Division, and Delimitation in a Colonial Town." Ph.D. diss., Boston College, 1975.

Tedesco, Paul H. "An Experiment in Labor Peace: Haverhill, Massachusetts, Shoe Workers, and Management, 1890-1930." 1984.

INDEX

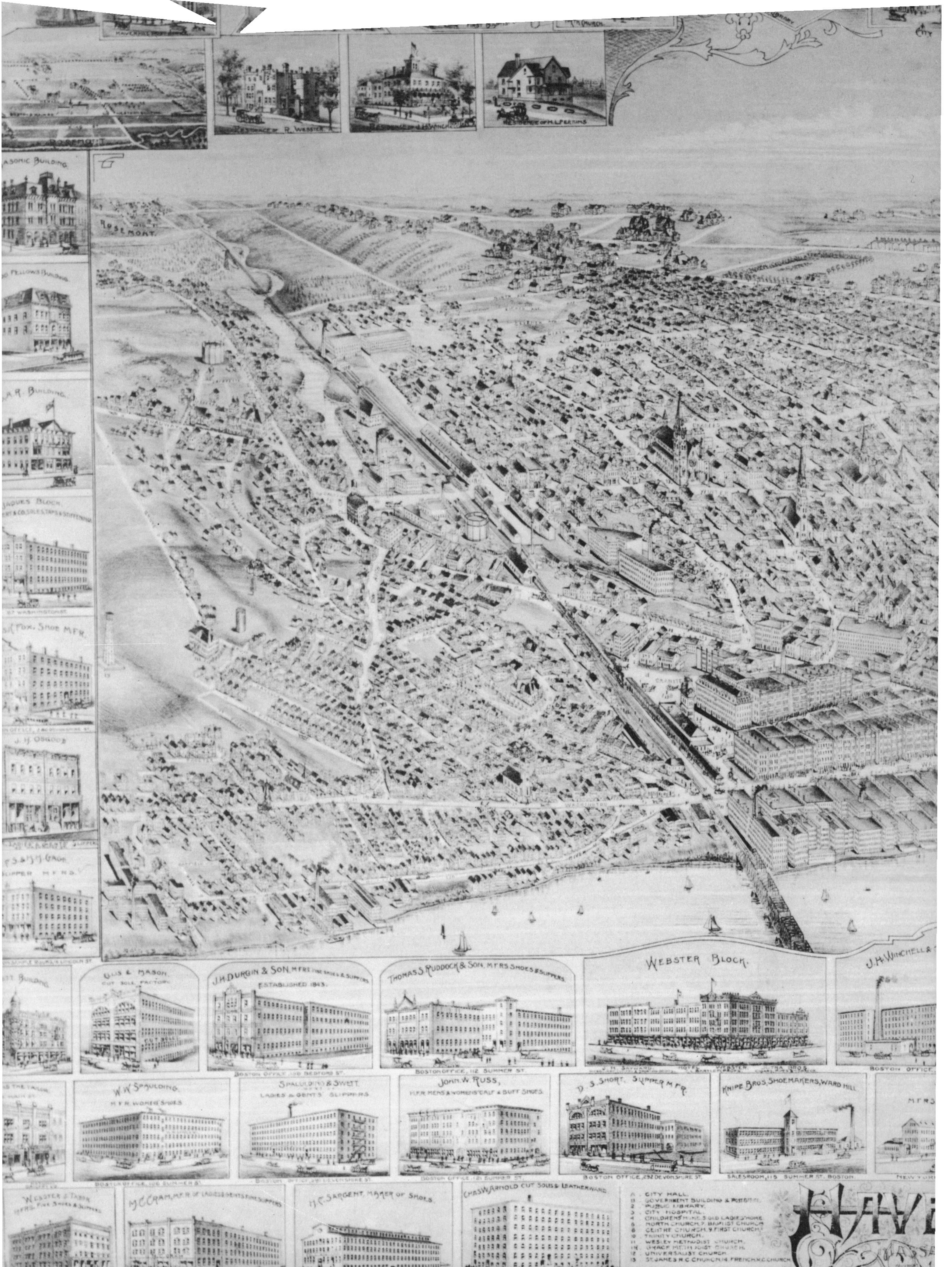

RESIDENCE OF R. WEBSTER
OLD OFFICE OF H.L. LEATHERS
MASONIC BUILDING
ODD FELLOWS BUILDING
G.A.R. BUILDING
JAQUES BLOCK
FOX SHOE MFR
J.H. OSGOOD
ROSEMONT
GEO. E. MASON, CUT SOLE FACTORY
J.H. DURGIN & SON, MFRS FINE SHOES & SLIPPERS. ESTABLISHED 1843.
THOMAS S. RUDDOCK & SON, MFRS SHOES & SLIPPERS
WEBSTER BLOCK
J.H. WINCHELL &
BOSTON OFFICE, 119 BEDFORD ST
BOSTON OFFICE, 112 SUMMER ST
W.W. SPAULDING, MFR WOMENS SHOES
SPAULDING & SWETT, LADIES & GENTS' SLIPPERS
JOHN W. RUSS, MFR MENS & WOMENS CALF & BUFF SHOES
D.S. SHORT, SLIPPER MFR
KNIPE BROS, SHOEMAKERS, WARD HILL
BOSTON OFFICE, 121 SUMMER ST
BOSTON OFFICE, 232 DEVONSHIRE ST
SALESROOM, 115 SUMMER ST. BOSTON
NEW YORK
WEBSTER & TABER, MFRS FINE SHOES & SLIPPERS
M.C. CRAM, MFR OF LADIES & GENTS FINE SLIPPERS
H.C. SARGENT, MAKER OF SHOES
CHAS W. ARNOLD, CUT SOLES & LEATHERBOARD
A. CITY HALL.
B. GOVERNMENT BUILDING & POST OFFICE.
1. PUBLIC LIBRARY.
2. CITY HOSPITAL.
3. CHILDRENS HOME & OLD LADIES' HOME.
4. NORTH CHURCH, 5. BAPTIST CHURCH.
6. CENTRE CHURCH, 7. FIRST CHURCH.
8. TRINITY CHURCH.
10. WESLEY METHODIST CHURCH.
11. GRACE METHODIST CHURCH.
12. UNIVERSALIST CHURCH.
13. ST. JAMES R.C. CHURCH, 14. FRENCH R.C. CHURCH.
HAVERHILL MASS.